1000 THINGS YOU SHOULD KNOW ABOUT

ANCIENT HISTORY

1000 THINGS YOU SHOULD KNOW ABOUT

ANCIENT HISTORY

John Farndon

Miles Kelly
PUBLISHING

First published in 2005 by Miles Kelly Publishing Ltd
Bardfield Centre, Great Bardfield, Essex, CM7 4SL

Copyright © Miles Kelly Publishing Ltd 2005

This title is also available in hardback

6 8 10 9 7 5

Editorial Director: Belinda Gallagher
Project Manager: Ian Paulyn
Production Manager: Estela Boulton
Written and designed: Barnsbury Books
Cover Designer: Tony Collins

British Library Cataloguing-in-Publication Data
A catalogue record for this book is available from the British library

ISBN 1-902947-77-0

Printed in China

info@mileskelly.net
visit us at our website: www.mileskelly.net

CONTENTS

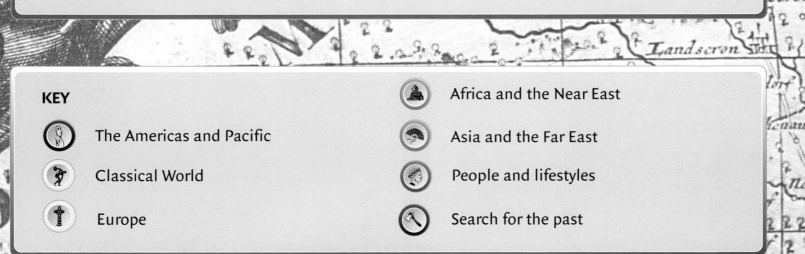

KEY

- The Americas and Pacific
- Classical World
- Europe
- Africa and the Near East
- Asia and the Far East
- People and lifestyles
- Search for the past

Origins of mankind

▼ Experts once thought humans evolved in a single line from australopiths, through Homo habilis (1), Homo erectus (2) and Neanderthal man (3) to humans (4). They now realize there were many branches.

- **Humans and apes** have so many similarities – such as long arms and fingers, and a big brain – most experts think they must have evolved from the same creature.

- **The common ancestor** may be four-legged orang-utan-like creatures called dryopithecines that lived in trees 22-10 million years ago (mya), like 'Proconsul' from E. Africa.

- **The break came when** 'hominids' (human-like apes) began to live on the ground and walk on two legs.

- **Footprints** of three bipedal (two-legged) creatures from 4 mya were found preserved in ash at Laetoli, Tanzania.

- **The oldest hominid** is called *Ardipithecus ramidus*, known from 4.4 mya bone fragments found in Aramis, Ethiopia.

- **Many very early** hominids are australopiths ('southern apes'), like the *Australopithecus anamensis* from 4.2 mya.

- **Australopiths** were only 1 m tall and their brain was about the same size as an ape's, but they were bipedal.

- **The best known** australopith is 'Lucy', a skeleton of *Australopithecus afarensis* of 3 mya, found in Kenya in 1974.

- **Lucy's discoverers** Don Johanson and Maurice Tieb called her Lucy because they were listening to the Beatles song 'Lucy in the Sky with Diamonds' at the time.

- **Many early hominid** remains are just skulls. Lucy was an almost complete skeleton. She showed that hominids learned to walk upright before their brains got bigger.

Handy Man

- **2.5-1.8 million years ago** the first really human-like hominids appeared. These hominids are all given the genus (group) name *Homo*, and include us.

- **The best known** early Homos are *Homo rudolfensis* and *Homo habilis*.

- **The first Homos** were taller than australopiths and had bigger brains.

- **Unlike australopiths,** Homos ate meat. They may have been forced to eat meat by a drying of the climate that cut the amount of plant food available.

- **Brains need** a lot of food, and eating meat gave the extra nourishment needed for bigger brains.

▶ Skulls show that the first Homos, like Homo habilis, had brains of 650 cubic cm (cc) – twice as big as australopiths. Ours are about 1,400 cc. But they had ape-like faces with protruding jaws and sloping foreheads.

- **Homo habilis** is known from bits of hand bones, a jaw and a skull found in Tanzania's Olduvai Gorge in 1961.

- **Homo habilis** means Handy Man. He gets his name because he has a good grip for wielding tools – with a thumb that can be rotated to meet the tip of a finger. This is called an 'opposable thumb'.

- **The first Homos** used bones or stones to break open bones to get at the marrow. Later they sharpened stones to cut meat for eating and hides for clothing. They may even have built simple shelters to live in.

- **Some experts** think the bulge in 'Broca's area' of some *Homo habilis* skulls suggests they could speak in a crude way. Most think they could not.

- **The first Homos** lived for a million or more years alongside 'robust' (bigger) australopiths, such as *Paranthropus boisei*.

Man the hunter

- **About 2 mya,** a much taller Homo called *Homo ergaster* appeared. Ergasters were the first creatures to have bodies much like ours, with long legs and straight backs.

- **Adult ergasters** were 1.6 m tall, weighed 65 kg and had brains of 850 cubic cm, well over half as big as ours.

- **Ergasters** did not just scavenge for meat like *Homo habilis*. They went hunting for large animals.

- **To hunt** and cut up meat, ergaster shaped stones, chipping flakes off to make proper double-edge blades or 'hand-axes'. Experts call this Acheulean tool-making.

- **To hunt effectively,** ergasters had to work together, so co-operation was the key to their success – and may have quickly led to the development of speech.

- **Ergasters** may have painted their bodies with red ochre.

> ★ STAR FACT ★
> Long legs and working together helped ergaster spread beyond Africa into Asia and maybe Europe.

▲ *Human development began when hominids learned to hunt together.*

- **Shortly after** ergaster came *Homo erectus* ('Upright Man').

- **Erectus** remains are found as far from Africa as Java. 700,000 year-old stone tools on the Indonesian island of Flores suggest they may have travelled by boat.

- **Erectus** learned to light fires, so they could live in colder places, and make a wider range of food edible by cooking.

Neanderthals and others

- **Hominids** appeared in Europe much later. The oldest, called *Homo antecessor*, dates from 800,000 years ago. This may have been a kind of erectus, or another species.

- **800-600,000 years ago** *Homo Heidelbergensis* appeared in Europe, Asia and Africa.

- **Heidelbergensis** may be a single species that came from Africa – or various species that evolved in different places.

- **Heidelbergensis** has many features in common with erectus, but is a major step on the way to modern humans with, for the first time, a brain as big as ours.

▶ *Most early hominid remains have been found in Africa. Many species – including modern humans – may have emerged first in Africa, then migrated elsewhere. These are sites where remains were found.*

- **Heidelbergensis** made good stone tools by making the core first, then shaping the blade with a single blow.

- **Heidelbergensis** was ancestor to Neanderthal Man, who lived in Europe from 250,000 to 30,000 years ago.

- **Neanderthals** were named after the Neander valley in Germany, where remains were found in 1856.

- **Neanderthals** were slightly shorter than modern humans but much stronger and with bigger brains. They must have been formidable hunters.

- **Neanderthals** buried their dead, often with tributes of flowers.

- **Neanderthals** lived in Croatia 28,000 years ago – long after modern humans. No one knows why they died out, leaving humans alone.

Swanscombe
Boxgrove
Les Eyzies
Grimaldi
Dolní Vestonice
Vindija, Croatia
Dmanisi
Shanidar
Skhul
Tabun
Bahr el Ghazal
Omo
Hadar (Lucy)
Nariokotome
Olduvai
Laetoli
Kabwe
Sterkfontein
Taung
Swartkrans
Klasies River

✤ Australopith, 1-4 mya
✤ H. habilis, 2.5-1 mya
✤ H. ergaster, 2-0.5 mya
✤ H. H'berg, 500-100,000 yrs
✤ N'thal 250-30,000 yrs
✤ H. sapiens 30,000 yrs

Modern humans

- **The scientific name** for modern humans is *Homo Sapiens Sapiens*. The word *Sapiens* is used twice to distinguish us from *Homo Sapiens Neanderthalis* (Neanderthal Man).

- **Unlike Neanderthals,** modern humans have a prominent chin and a flat face with a high forehead.

- **Some scientists** think the similarity of DNA in our bodies means all humans are descended from a woman nicknamed 'Eve', who they calculate lived in Africa about 200,000 years ago. DNA is the special molecule in every body-cell that carries the body's instructions for life.

- **The oldest human skulls** are 130,000 years old and were found in the Omo Basin in Ethiopia and the Klasies river in South Africa.

- **About 30,000 years ago** modern humans began to spread out into Eurasia from Africa.

- **The earliest modern Europeans** are called Cro-Magnon Man, after the caves in France's Dordogne valley where skeletons from 35,000 years ago were found in 1868.

- **Modern humans** reached Australia by boat from Indonesia 50,000 years ago. They reached the Americas from Asia about the same time.

- **Modern humans** lived alongside Neanderthals for tens of thousands of years in the Middle East and Europe.

- **Modern humans** were probably the first creatures to speak what we would call language. Some scientists think language was a sudden genetic accident which gave humans a huge advantage.

- **With modern humans** came rapid advances in stone-tool technology, the building of wooden huts, a rise in population and a growing interest in art.

◄ *Both modern humans and Neanderthals used beautifully made spears for hunting.*

Cave painters

- **Prehistoric people** sometimes lived in caves, but more often they went into caves to paint and draw.

- **The world's** most famous cave paintings, at Lascaux in France and Altamira in Spain, were found by children.

- **Carbon dating** shows the paintings in Lascaux are 31,000 years old. Those in Chauvet in the French Ardèche are nearly twice as old.

- **The pictures** at Cougnac in France were painted over a period of 10,000 years.

- **Most paintings** in caves show large animals such as bison, deer, horses and mammoths.

- **Caves** may have been the temples of prehistoric times, and the paintings linked to religious rituals.

- **Cave artists** often painted by spitting paint, just as Australian aboriginals do today.

- **To reach** the 14,000-year-old paintings in France's Pergouset, you must crawl through 150 m of passages.

- **In the caves** at Nerja in Spain there are rock formations that prehistoric people played like a xylophone.

- **The aboriginal paintings** on rocks in Arnhemland, Northern Territory, Australia may be over 50,000 years old.

◄ *The most famous cave paintings are those in the Hall of Bulls at Lascaux in France. These paintings show bison.*

The Stone Ages

- **The Stone Ages** were the ages before humans discovered metals and so used mainly stones for making tools.

- **Stone tools** were made by chipping away stones to make hammers, spear and arrow heads, knives and scrapers.

- **People usually** used local stone, but sometimes good stones were imported from long distances.

- **Early Europeans** used mainly flint. Africans used quartz, chert, basalt and obsidian.

- **In Europe** there were three Stone Ages : Old (Palaeolithic), Middle (Mesolithic) and New (Neolithic).

▶ *Mesolithic people hunted with bows and arrows and flint-tipped spears.*

- **The Palaeolithic** began 2 million years ago when various human ancestors gathered plants and hunted with stone weapons.

- **The Mesolithic** was the transition from the Old to the New Stone Age – after the Last Ice Age ended around 12,000 years ago.

- **The Neolithic** was the time when people began to settle down and farm. This occurred first in the Near East, about 10,000 years ago.

- **In 1981,** a pebble shaped into a female form, half a million years old was found at Berekhat Ram in Israel's Golan Heights.

- **Venus figurines** are plump stone female figures from c.25,000 years ago, found in Europe, e.g. the Czech Republic.

The Bronze Age

- **The Bronze Age** is the period of prehistory when people first began to use the metal bronze.

- **Bronze** is an alloy (mix) of copper with about 10% tin.

- **The first metals used** were probably lumps of pure gold and copper, beaten into shape to make ornaments in Turkey and Iran about 6000BC.

- **Metal ores** (metals mixed with other minerals) were probably discovered when certain stones were found to melt when heated in a kiln.

- **Around 4000BC,** metal smiths in southeast Europe and Iran began making copper axeheads with a central hole to take a wooden shaft.

- **The Copper Age** is the period when people used copper before they learned to alloy it with tin to make bronze. Metalworking with copper was flourishing in the early cities of Mesopotamia, in the Middle East, about 3500BC.

- **The Bronze Age** began several times between 3500 and 3000BC in the Near East, Balkans and

SE Asia when smiths discovered that, by adding a small quantity of tin, they could make bronze. Bronze is harder than copper and easier to make into a sharp blade.

- **Knowledge of bronze** spread slowly across Eurasia, but by 1500BC it was in use all the way from Europe to India.

- **The rarity of tin** spurred long-distance trade links – and the first mines, like the tin mines in Cornwall, England.

- **Bronze** can be cast – shaped by melting it into a clay mould (itself shaped with a wax model). For the first time people could make things any shape they wanted. Skilled smiths across Eurasia began to cast bronze to make everything from weapons to cooking utensils.

◀ *By 1000BC, beautiful metal swords and other weapons with sharp blades like this were being made all over Europe and western Asia.*

The Iron Age

► Maiden Castle in Dorset is the largest of around 1,000 hillforts built in southern Britain in the Iron Age. This is how it might have looked in about 300BC.

Typical Iron Age round houses, built of wood, and straw thatch

The hilltop village within the defences covered about 17 hectares

The inner rampart was 14 m high and topped by a fence of huge, upright timbers. It was faced with big limestone blocks, not grass

A series of ditches and banks were built up from clay

The entrance wound between ramparts to make life hard for attackers

The entrance through the inner ramparts had massive timber gates

► The cheapness and availability of iron in the Iron Age meant that even quite a poor man might have his own sword.

- **The Iron Age** is the time in prehistory when iron replaced bronze as the main metal.

- **The use of iron** was discovered by the Hittites in Anatolia, Turkey between 1500 and 1200BC. This discovery helped to make the Hittites immensely powerful for a few centuries.

- **Around 1200BC,** the Hittite Empire collapsed and the use of iron spread through Asia and central Europe. The Dorian Greeks became famous iron masters.

- **Tin is rare**, so bronze objects were made mostly for chieftains. Iron ore is common, so ordinary people could have metal objects such as cooking utensils.

- **Many ordinary farmers** could afford iron scythes and axes. With tough metal tools to clear fields and harvest crops quickly, farming developed much more rapidly.

- **Growth in population** put pressure on resources and warfare increased across Eurasia. Partly as a result, many northern Europe settlements developed into hillforts – hilltop sites protected by earth ramparts, ditches and stockades.

- **Around 650BC,** peoples skilled in iron working called Celts began to dominate northern Europe.

- **Iron working** reached China around 600BC. The Chinese used large bellows to boost furnace temperatures enough to melt ore in large quantities.

- **Iron tools** appearing in West Africa around 400BC were the basis of the Nok culture. Nok farmers speaking Bantu spread south and east all over Africa.

> ★ STAR FACT ★
> In 1950, an Iron Age man was found in a peatbog at Tollund in Jutland, Denmark, perfectly preserved over 2,000 years.

Megaliths

- **Megalith** means 'giant stone'.

- **Megaliths** are monuments such as tombs made from huge blocks of stone, built in western Europe in the Neolithic and Bronze Ages between 4000 and 1500BC.

- **It was once** thought megaliths began in one place. Now experts think they emerged in many areas.

- **Menhirs** are large standing stones. Sometimes they stand by themselves, sometimes in avenues or circles.

- **The largest** known menhir is the Grand Menhir Brisé at Locmariaquer near Carnac, France. This single stone once stood 20 m tall and weighed 280 tonnes.

- **The largest stone circle** is at Avebury in Wiltshire.

- **The most famous stone circle** is Stonehenge on Salisbury Plain, built between 2950 and 1600BC.

> ★ STAR FACT ★
> The Grand Menhir Brisé is seven times as heavy as the biggest stones at Stonehenge.

▲ The most famous avenues of stone are at Carnac in Brittany, France, where thousands of stones stand in long lines.

- **Some megaliths** align with amazing accuracy with astronomical events, such as sunrise at the solstice (midsummer day) and may have acted as calendars.

- **Erecting the stones** took huge teams of men working with wooden rollers, levers and ropes.

Archaeology

- **Archaeology** is the scientific study of relics left by humans in the past, from old bones to ancient temples.

- **Most archeological relics** are buried beneath the ground or sunk beneath the sea.

- **Aerial photography** often shows places to dig. Crops and grass will grow differently if the soil is affected by a buried wall or filled-in ditch.

- **Geophysical surveys** involve using metal detectors and other electronic probes to pick up features underground.

- **Field walking** involves walking over the site, carefully scanning the ground by eye for tiny relics.

▶ Archeological digging is a very painstaking process. Diggers must work with immense care to avoid missing or breaking tiny, fragile relics.

- **During a dig,** archaeologists dig carefully down through the layers, noting exactly where every relic was found, in case their position helps to reveal the story.

- **Archaeologists** call on many different kinds of expert to help them interpret finds. Forensic scientists may help tell how a skeleton died, for instance.

- **The deeper** a relic is buried, the older it is likely to be.

- **Radio carbon dating** is a way of dating the remains of once-living things from their carbon content. This is accurate up to 50,000 years ago.

- **Potassium argon dating** helps to date the rocks in which relics were found from their potassium and argon content. Human remains in Africa were dated this way.

The first farms

▲ Farming began about 11,000 years ago as people began saving grass seed to grow, so they could grind new seed into flour.

- **Starch marks** on stone implements found in Papua New Guinea suggest yams may have been grown there at least 30,000 years ago.

- **Water chestnuts** and beans may have been farmed near Spirit Cave in north Vietnam from 11,000 to 7,500BC.

- **About 9000BC,** some people abandoned the old way of life, hunting animals and gathering fruit, and settled down to farm in what is called the Neolithic Revolution.

- **Farming began** as people planted grasses for their seed (or grain) in the Near East, in Guangdong in China and in Latin America – and perhaps planted root vegetables in Peru and Indonesia too.

- **Emmer wheat and barley** were grown in the Near East c.8,000BC. Sheep and goats were tamed here soon after.

- **The ox-drawn plough** was used from c.5000BC. The Chinese used hand ploughs even earlier.

- **Crop irrigation canals** were dug at Choya Mami, near Mandali in Iraq, between 5500 and 4750BC.

- **China,** the Indus, Egypt and Babylonia all had extensive irrigation systems by 3000BC.

- **The first farmers** reaped their grain with sickles of flint.

- **Farmers** soon learned to store food. Underground granaries at Ban-Po, Shansi, China, date from c.4800BC.

The first cities

- **The walls** of the city of Jericho on the River Jordan are 11,000 years old, and the city has been continuously occupied longer than anywhere else in the world.

- **People began** to live in towns when farming produced enough extra food for people to specialize in crafts such as basket-making and for people to begin to trade.

- **Villages and towns** probably first developed in the Near East in the Neolithic, about 8000BC.

- **Tells** are mounds built up at ancient settlement sites in the Near and Middle East as mud-brick houses crumble.

- **The most famous** ancient town is Catal Hüyük in Anatolia, in Turkey, which was occupied from 7000 to 5500BC. 10,000 people may have lived here.

- **The houses** in Catal Hüyük were made from mud bricks covered with fine plaster. Some rooms were shrines, with bulls' heads and mother goddesses.

- **Asikli Hüyük** is a nearby forerunner of Catal Hüyük, dating from over a thousand years earlier.

- **The first big city** was Eridu in Mesopotamia (Iraq's Abu Shahrain Tell) which has a temple dating from 4900BC.

- **50,000 people** were living in Sumerian Uruk (modern Warka) on the banks of the Euphrates in Iraq in 3500BC.

- **Sumerian Ur** was the first city to have a population of a quarter of a million, by about 2500BC.

◀ Houses in Catal Hüyük were so tightly packed people had to walk over flat roofs to get to them, then climb through a hole down ladders.

Mesopotamia and Sumer

- **Mesopotamia** lies between the Tigris and Euphrates Rivers in Turkey, Syria and Iraq. *Mesopotamia* is Greek for 'between rivers'.

- **Mesopotamia** is called the 'cradle of civilization' because many ancient civilizations arose here, including the Sumerian, Babylonian and Assyrian.

- **The first great civilization** was that of the Sumerians, who farmed irrigated land by the Euphrates c.5000BC and lived in mud-brick houses.

- **By 4000BC,** the settlements of Eridu, Uruk and Ur had grown into towns with water supplies and drainage systems, palaces and temple mounds called ziggurats.

- **Sumerians** devised the first writing system (cuneiform), made with wedge-shaped marks on clay tablets.

◄ *No one knows when the wheel was invented. It probably developed from potters' wheels. But by 3200BC carts like this were used in Sumer.*

- **Sumerians** cast beautiful objects – first from copper, then, from 3500BC, in bronze.

- **The Sumerian** *Epic of Gilgamesh* tells of a flood similar to the biblical story of Noah's Ark.

- **The Sumerians** developed the first elaborate systems of government and law.

- **At first each city** or 'city-state' was run by a council of elders, but in wartime a *lugal* (leader) took charge. By 2900BC *lugals* were kings and ruled all the time.

- **In 2350BC** Sumer was overrun by Sargon of Akkad, but Sumerian power was re-established at Ur in 2150BC.

Indus civilization

★ **STAR FACT** ★
Soapstone trading seals from the Indus have been found as far away as Bahrain and Ur.

- **About 3000BC** a civilization developed from small farming communities in the Indus valley in Pakistan.

- **The remains** of over 100 towns of the Indus civilization have been found. The main sites are Mohenjo-Daro, Harappa, Kalibangan and Lothal.

- **Indus cities** were carefully planned, with straight streets, bath-houses and big granaries.

- **At the centre** was a fortified citadel, built on a platform of bricks. The rulers probably lived here.

- **Indus houses** were built of brick around a central courtyard. They had several rooms, a toilet and a well.

- **The Indus civilization** had its own system of writing, which appears on objects such as carved seals – but no one has yet been able to decipher it.

▶ *Seals like this were used by Indus merchants to stamp bales of goods.*

- **Single-room** huts at all intersections are thought to be police-posts.

- **Mohenjo-Daro** and Harappa had 35,000 inhabitants each by about 2500BC.

- **By 1750BC** the Indus civilization had declined, perhaps because floods changed the course of the Indus River. War may also have played a part. It finally vanished with the arrival of the Aryans in India about 1500BC.

Great migrations

- **The first migrations** occurred when human-like *Homo ergaster* walked out of Africa 750,000 years ago (ya).

- **Experts once** thought oceans blocked migrations but it now seems boats have been used since the earliest days.

- **100,000 ya** humans moved out of Africa into the Near East.

- **About 50,000 ya** humans began the great expansion that took them to every continent but Antarctica within 20,000 years – and wiped out the Neanderthals.

- **50-40,000 ya,** humans spread across Asia and Australasia. 40-35,000 ya, they moved into Europe. 30-25,000 ya, they trekked out of northeast Asia and crossed into the Americas.

- **Early humans** were mainly nomadic hunters, always on the move, following animals into empty lands.

- **Changes in climate** triggered many migrations. People moved north in warm times and retreated in Ice Ages. When the last Ice Age ended, 10,000 ya, hunters moved north through Europe as the weather warmed. Those left behind in the Middle East settled down to farm.

- **From 9,000-7,000 ya**, farming spread northwest through Europe – partly through people actually moving, partly by word of mouth.

- **4,000 ya,** Indo-European peoples spread out from their home in southern Russia. They went south into Iran (as Mittanians) and India (Aryans), southwest into Turkey (Hittites) and Greece (Mycenaeans) and west (Celts).

- **About 3,000 ya,** the Sahara began to dry up, and people living there moved to the fringes. Bantu people from Nigeria and the Congo spread south through Africa.

▶ *Just like American pioneers in the 1800s, Aryans 4,000 years ago moved their families and possessions in covered wagons, probably pulled by oxen.*

The beginnings of Egypt

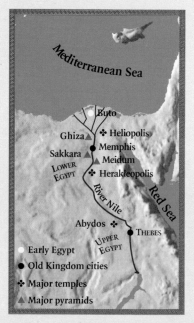

▲ *The Ancient Egyptians built great cities and monuments along the Nile Valley during the Old Kingdom.*

- **While dozens** of cities were developing in Mesopotamia, in Egypt the foundations were being laid for the first great nation.

- **From 5000-3300BC** farmers by the River Nile banded together to dig canals to control the Nile's annual flooding and water their crops.

- **By 3300BC,** Nile farming villages had grown into towns. Rich and powerful kings were buried in big, box-like mud-brick tombs called *mastabas*.

- **Egyptian townspeople** began to work copper and stone, paint vases, weave baskets and use potters' wheels.

- **Early Egypt** was divided into two kingdoms: Upper Egypt, and Lower Egypt on the Nile delta. In 3100BC, King Menes of Upper Egypt conquered Lower Egypt to unite the two kingdoms, but a king of Egypt was always called King of Upper and Lower Egypt.

- **Menes** founded a capital for united Egypt at Memphis.

- **With Menes**, Egypt's Dynasty I – the first family of kings – began. The time of Dynasties I and II, which lasted until 2649BC, is known as the Archaic Period.

- **After the Archaic Period** came the Old Kingdom (2649-2134BC), perhaps the greatest era of Egyptian culture.

- **Craftsmen** made fine things, scholars developed writing and the calendar and studied astronomy and maths.

- **The greatest scholar** and priest was Imhotep, minister to King Zoser (2630-2611BC). Imhotep was architect of the first of the great pyramids, the Step Pyramid at Sakkara.

Babylon

- **Babylon** was one of the greatest cities of the ancient world. It stood on the banks of the Euphrates River, near what is now Al Hillah in Iraq.

- **Babylon** reached its peak in two phases: the Old Babylonian Empire (1792-1234BC) and the New Babylonian Empire (626-539BC).

- **Babylon first** grew as a city from 2200BC, but only when Hammurabi became king in 1792 did it become powerful. In his 42-year reign, Hammurabi's conquests gave Babylon a huge empire in Mesopotamia.

- **Hammurabi** was a great law-maker, and some of his laws were enscribed on a stone pillar, or stele, now in the Louvre in Paris. One of his main laws was that 'the strong shall not oppress the weak'. There were also strong laws to punish crimes and protect people from poor workmanship by builders and doctors.

- **After Hammurabi died,** Babylonian power declined and the Assyrians gained the upper hand. After long Babylonian resistance, the Assyrians destroyed the city in 689BC, only to rebuild it 11 years later.

- ◀ Under Nebuchadnezzar II (630-562BC), Babylon achieved its greatest fame. He is known for conquering Jerusalem and for his great building projects.

- **Just 60 years or so later,** Babylonian king Nabopolassar and his son Nebuchadnezzar II crushed the Assyrians and built the new Babylonian Empire.

- **Under Nebuchadnezzar II,** Babylon became a vast, magnificent city of 250,000 people, with grand palaces, temples and houses.

- **Babylon** was surrounded by walls 26 m thick – glazed with blue bricks, decorated with dragons, lions and bulls and pierced by eight huge bronze gates. The grandest gate was the Ishtar Gate, which opened on to a paved avenue called the Processional Street.

- **Babylonians** were so sure of their power that King Belshazzar was having a party when the Persians, led by Cyrus, attacked. Cyrus's men dug canals to divert the Euphrates river, then slipped into the city along the river bed.

> ★ **STAR FACT** ★
> Dying of a fever, Alexander the Great found cool relief in the Hanging Gardens.

▶ The Greeks described the Hanging Gardens of Babylon as one of the Seven Wonders of the ancient world. Nebuchadnezzar II was said to have had them built for his wife Amyitis, who missed the greenery of her mountain home.

Gardens of lush trees and flowers filled rising brick terraces

The gardens were on a huge pyramid of brick and tar, 25 m high

Water for the plants was continually raised from the river by screw pumps wound by slaves

First Chinese emperors

- **In China,** farming communities known as the Yanshao culture developed by the Huang He (Yellow River) 7,000 years ago. By 5000BC, the region was ruled by emperors.

- **Early Chinese emperors** are known of only by legend. Huang-Ti, the Yellow Emperor, was said to have become emperor in 2697BC.

- **In about 2690BC,** Huang-Ti's wife, Hsi-Ling Shi, discovered how to use the cocoon of the silkworm (the caterpillar of the *Bombyx mori* moth) to make silk. Hsi-Ling was afterwards known as Seine-Than (the Silk Goddess).

- **By 2000BC,** the Chinese were making beautiful jade carvings.

▶ *The Shang emperors were warriors. Their soldiers fought in padded bamboo armour.*

- **The Hsias family** were said to be one of the earliest dynasties of Chinese emperors, ruling from 2000 to 1750BC.

- **The Shangs** were the first definitely known dynasty of emperors. They came to power in 1750BC.

- **Shang emperors** had their fortune told every few days from cracks on heated animal bones. Marks on these 'oracle' bones are the oldest examples of Chinese writing.

- **Under the Shangs,** the Chinese became skilled bronze casters.

- **In the Shang cities** of Anyang and Zengzhou, thick-walled palace temples were surrounded at a distance by villages of artisans.

- **Shang emperors** went to their tombs along with their servants and captives as well as entire chariots with their horses and drivers.

Egyptian writing

- **Ancient Egyptian** writing developed between 3300 and 3100BC – perhaps inspired by Sumerian scripts.

- **Egyptian writing** is called hieroglyphic (Greek for 'holy writing'). The Egyptians called it the 'words of the gods', because they believed writing was given by the god Thoth.

- **The last known** hieroglyphs were written in AD394, long after anyone knew how to read them.

- **In AD1799,** the French soldiers of Napoleon's army found a stone slab at Rosetta in Egypt. It was covered in three identical texts.

- **In AD1822,** Jean François Champollion deciphered the Rosetta stone, realizing that hieroglyphs are pictures that stand for sounds and letters, not just for objects.

- **There are 700** hieroglyphs. Most are pictures and can be written from left to right, right to left or downwards.

- **Words inside** an oval shape called a *cartouche* are the names of pharaohs.

- **There were two short-hand** versions of hieroglyphs for everyday use – early hieratic script and later demotic script.

- **Egyptians** not only wrote on tomb walls but wrote everyday things with ink and brushes on papyrus (paper made from papyrus reeds) or ostraca (pottery fragments).

- **Only highly trained** scribes could write. Scribes were very well paid and often exempt from taxes.

◀ *The walls of Egyptian tombs are covered in hieroglyphs.*

Egyptian lifestyles

▲ Egyptian girls were highly conscious of their looks, wearing make-up and jewellery and doing their hair carefully.

- **Egyptian women** painted their nails with henna and reddened their lips and cheeks with red ochre paste.
- **Egyptian fashions** changed little over thousands of years, and their clothes were usually white linen.
- **Men wrapped linen** round themselves in a kilt. Women wore long, light dresses. Children ran naked in summer.
- **Every Egyptian** wore jewellery. The rich wore gold inlaid with gems; the poor wore copper or faience (made by heating powdered quartz).
- **Egyptians** loved board games. The favourites were *senet* and 'hounds and jackals'.
- **Rich Egyptians** had lavish parties with food and drink, singers, musicians, acrobats and dancing girls.
- **Rich Egyptians** often went fishing or boating.

- **Egyptians** washed every day in the river or with a jug and basin. The rich were given showers by servants.
- **Instead of soap** they used a cleansing cream made from oil, lime and perfume. They also rubbed themselves all over with moisturizing oil.

Ancient Crete

- **The Minoan civilization** of Crete – an island south of Greece – was the first civilization in Europe.
- **Minoan civilization** began about 3000BC, reached its height from 2200 to 1450BC, then mysteriously vanished – perhaps after the volcano on nearby Santorini erupted.
- **The name Minoan** comes from the Greek legend of King Minos. Minos was the son of Europa, the princess seduced by the god Zeus in the shape of a bull.
- **Greek stories** tell how Minos built a labyrinth (maze) in which he kept the Minotaur, a monster with a man's body and a bull's head.
- **Catching a bull** by the horns and leaping over it (bull-leaping) was an important Minoan religious rite.
- **Experts now think Minos** was a title, so every Cretan king was called Minos.
- **The Minoans** were great seafarers and traded all over the eastern Mediterranean.
- **At the centre** of each Minoan town was a palace, such as those found at Knossos, Zakro, Phaestos and Mallia.
- **The largest Minoan palace** is at Knossos, which covered 20,000 square metres and housed over 30,000 people.
- **The walls** of the palace are decorated with frescoes (paintings), which reveal a great deal about the Minoans.

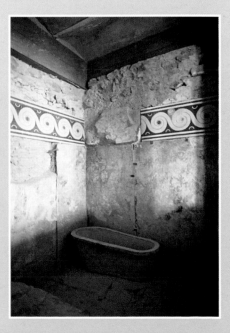

▶ Knossos had a very good water supply system via long clay pipes. This is the queen's bathroom.

The pharaohs

Family shrine

Grand reception area where the official did his business for the pharaoh

Well

The central hall was where the official entertained friends

Bedrooms

Kitchen

Wine cellar

Servants' quarters

Stables

Grain stores

▶ The patronage of the pharaohs gave great power and prestige to their officials, who built houses like these around 1200BC.

★ STAR FACT ★
People thought the pharaoh could control the weather and make the land fertile.

- **Pharaohs** were the kings of Ancient Egypt. They were also High Priest, head judge and commander of the army.

- **Egyptians** thought of the pharaoh as both the god Horus and the son of the sun god Re. When he died he was transformed into the god Osiris, father of Horus. Since he was a god, anyone approaching him had to crawl.

- **The pharaoh was** thought to be so holy that he could not be addressed directly. Instead, people referred to him indirectly by talking of the pharaoh, which is Egyptian for 'great house'. Only after about 945BC was he addressed directly as the pharaoh.

- **In official documents** the pharaoh had five titles: Horus; Two Ladies; Golden Horus; King of Upper and Lower Egypt and Lord of the Double Land (Upper and Lower Egypt); and Son of Re and Lord of the Diadems.

- **The pharaoh's godlike** status gave him magical powers. His *uraeus* (the snake on his crown) was supposed to spit flames at his enemies and he could trample thousands.

- **There were 31 dynasties** (families) of pharaohs, beginning with Menes in c.3100BC and ending with the Persian kings in 323BC. Each dynasty is identified in order by a Roman numeral. So the fifth Dynasty is Dynasty V.

- **A pharaoh** usually married his eldest sister to keep the royal blood pure. She became queen and was known as the Royal Heiress, but the pharaoh had many other wives. If the pharaoh died while his eldest son was still a child, his queen became regent and ruled on his behalf.

- **To preserve their bodies for ever,** pharaohs were buried inside massive tombs. The first pharaohs were buried in huge pyramids. Because these were often robbed, later pharaohs were buried in tombs cut deep into cliffs.

- **One of the greatest pharaohs** was Ramses II, who ruled from 1290 to 1224BC. He left a legacy of many huge buildings including the rock temple of Abu Simbel.

The Olmecs and Chavins

- **People** began farming in Meso America (Mexico and Central America) 9,000 years ago, almost as long ago as in the Middle East.

- **By 2000BC** there were permanent villages and large farms growing corn, beans, squash and other crops.

- **Between 1200 and 400BC,** a remarkable culture was developed by the Olmecs in western Mexico.

- **The Olmecs** had a counting system and calendar, but no writing system, so little is known about them.

- **Ruins of a huge** Olmec pyramid have been found at La Venta in Tabasco, Mexico.

- **The Olmecs** carved huge 'baby-face' heads from basalt with enormous skill – apparently with only stone chisels, since they had no metal.

- **By 2000BC,** huge religious sites were being built all over what is now Peru.

- **From 800 to 400BC,** the Chavin civilization spread from the religious centre of Chavin de Huantar in the Peruvian mountains.

- **From AD100 to 700,** America's first true city developed at Teotihuacan, with vast pyramids and palaces.

- **Teotihuacan** may have been the world's biggest city in AD300, with a population of over 250,000.

◄ The Olmec heads were carved from huge blocks of volcanic rock weighing up to 14 tonnes. No one knows how they were moved.

Aryan India

- **The Aryans** were a fair-skinned herding people from southern Russia, ancestors to both Greeks and Indians.

- **About 2000BC,** the Aryan people began to sweep through Persia and on into India, where they destroyed the Indus civilizations.

- **The Aryans** were tough warriors who loved music, dancing and chariot racing, but slowly adopted Dravidian gods and settled in villages as farmers.

- **Aryans** were originally split into three classes: Brahmins (priests) at the top, Kshatriya (warriors) in the middle and Vaisyas (merchants and farmers) at the bottom.

- **When they settled** in India, the Aryans added a fourth class, the conquered, dark-skinned Dravidians, who became their servants.

- **From the four Aryan classes,** the elaborate system of castes (classes) in today's India developed.

- **The Aryans** gave India Sanskrit, the ancestor of all India's languages today.

- **Sanskrit** is closely related to European languages such as English, German and Latin.

- **The Aryans** had no form of writing, but they passed on history and religion by word of mouth in spoken Books of Knowledge, or *Vedas.*

- **The Brahmins** created as *Vedas* the first Hindu scriptures, including the *Rig-Veda,* the *Sama-Veda* and *Yajur-Veda.*

► The dark-skinned Dravidian people who lived in India when the Aryans arrived became the servant class.

Semites

- **Jewish people** and Arabs are Semitic people.

- **In 2500BC,** the Semites were farming peoples such as the Akkadians, Canaanites and Amorites, who lived in what is now Israel, Jordan and Syria.

- **In 2371BC,** an Akkadian called Sargon seized the throne of the Sumerian city of Kish. He soon conquered all Sumer and Akkad and created a great empire.

- **The Akkadian Empire** collapsed c.2230BC, under attacks from tribes of Gutians from the mountains.

- **From 3000 to 1500BC,** Canaanite Byblos was one of the world's great trading ports, famous for its purple cloth.

- **c.2000BC,** Amorites conquered Sumer, Akkad and Canaan. In 1792BC, the Amorite Hammurabi was ruler of Babylon.

◄ *The Dead Sea Scrolls, on display here, are ancient Hebrew manuscripts found by shepherds in 1947 in a cave near the Dead Sea. They include the oldest known texts of the Bible's Old Testament.*

- **The first Hebrews** were a Semitic tribe from southern Mesopotamia. Their name meant 'people of the other side' of the Euphrates River.

- **According** to the Bible, the first Hebrew was Abraham, a shepherd who lived in the Sumerian city of Ur, 4,000 years ago. He led his family first to Syria, then to Canaan (now Palestine), where he settled.

- **Abraham's grandson** Jacob was also called Israel and the Hebrews were afterwards called Israelites.

- **About 1000BC,** the Israelites prospered under three kings – Saul, David and Solomon.

The Assyrians

- **The Assyrians** came originally from the upper Tigris valley around the cities of Ashur, Nineveh and Arbela.

- **c.2000BC,** Assyria was invaded by Amorites. Under a line of Amorite kings, Assyria built up a huge empire. King Adadnirari I called himself 'King of Everything'.

- **The Old Assyrian Empire** lasted six centuries, until it was broken up by horsemen from a place called Mittani.

★ STAR FACT ★
King Assurbanipal's (668-627BC) palace was filled with books and plants from all over the world.

- **From 1114 to 1076BC,** King Tiglath Pileser I rebuilt Assyrian power by conquest, creating the New Assyrian Empire.

- **The New Assyrian Empire** reached its peak under Tiglath-Pileser III (744-727BC) and was finally overthrown by the Medes and Babylonians in 612BC.

- **The Assyrians** were ruthless warriors. They grew beards and fought with bows, iron swords, spears and chariots.

- **The Assyrians** built good roads all over their empire, so that the army could move fast to quell trouble.

- **The Assyrians** built magnificent palaces and cities such as Khorsabad and Nimrud.

- **Arab warriors** rode camels into battle for the Assyrians.

◄ *Statues of winged bulls with human heads were found at Nimrud.*

Oceania

- **The people** of the Pacific may have been the greatest seafarers of the ancient world.

- **Up until 5,000 years ago,** the sea was lower and Tasmania, Australia and New Guinea were all part of one big continent.

- **About 50,000 years ago,** bold, seafaring people crossed the ocean from Southeast Asia and settled in Australia.

- **Most early sites** are now lost offshore under the sea, which rose to cut off New Guinea and Australia c.5000BC.

- **The Australian** aboriginals are descendants of these original inhabitants.

- **The oldest settlement** in New Guinea is 40,000 years old.

- **c.4000BC,** domesticated plants and animals reached New Guinea from Asia, and farmers drained fields at Kuk Swamp. But many people remained hunters.

- **About 2000BC,** people sailed in canoes from Indonesia to colonize Melanesia and Micronesia – the islands of the western Pacific, such as Vanuatu.

▲ *The people of Oceania crossed the oceans in canoes like these tens of thousands of years before the great European explorers.*

- **Early Melanesians** are known by their 'Lapita' pottery, which originated in the Molucca Islands of Indonesia.

- **Rowing canoes** seen in a 50,000-year-old cave painting in Australia match those seen all over the Pacific – and in caves in the Amazon jungle.

Dead Egyptians

- **Egyptians saw death** as a step on the way to a fuller life in the Next World.

- **Everyone was thought** to have three souls: the *ka*, *ba* and *akh*. For these to be well, the body must survive intact, so the Egyptians tried to preserve the body.

- **Gradually,** the Egyptians developed embalming techniques to preserve the bodies of kings and rich people who could afford it.

- **The organs** were cut out and stored in 'canopic jars' and the body dried with natron (salt).

- **The dried body** was filled with sawdust, resin and natron, then wrapped in bandages. The embalmed body is a 'mummy'.

- **A portrait** mask was put over the mummy's head, then it was put in a coffin.

- **Anthropoid (human-shaped)** coffins were used from about 2000BC onwards. Often, the mummy was put inside a nest of two or three coffins, each carved and painted and perhaps decorated with gold and gems.

- **The wooden coffin** was laid inside a stone coffin or sarcophagus inside the burial chamber.

- **At first,** the prayers said for a dead ruler were carved on pyramid walls as 'Pyramid Texts'. Later, they were put on coffins as 'Coffin Texts'. From 1500BC, they were written on papyrus in the *Book of the Dead*.

- **To help him** overcome various tests and make it to the Next World, a dead man needed amulets and a *Book of the Dead*, containing magic spells and a map.

◄ *When placing the mask over the mummy, the chief embalmer wore a mask representing the jackal god Anubis.*

Persia

- **Iran** is named after the Aryan people who began settling there in c.15,000BC. Two Aryan tribes – the Medes and Persians – soon became dominant.

- **In 670BC,** the Medes under King Cyaxeres joined forces with the Babylonians to finally overthrow the Assyrians.

- **In 550BC,** the Medes themselves were overthrown by the Persians. The Persian king Cyrus II was the grandson of the king of the Medes, Astyages.

- **Cyrus II** had an army of horsemen and very skilled archers. He went on to establish a great Persian empire after conquering Lydia and Babylon.

- **The Persian Empire** was ruled by the Achaemenid family until it was destroyed by Alexander the Great in 330BC.

◄ *Darius the Great ruled Persia from 521 until 486BC.*

- **The Persian Empire** reached its greatest extent under Darius I, who called himself Shahanshah ('King of kings'). Darius introduced gold and silver coins, and also brought chickens to the Middle East.

- **Darius built** a famous road system and split his empire into 20 *satrapies* (regions), each ruled by a *satrap*.

- **'King's Ears'** were officials who travelled around and reported trouble back to the king.

- **The Persians** built luxurious cities and palaces, first at Susa, then in Darius's reign, at Persepolis.

- **Persian priests,** or magi, were known for their magic skills, and gave us the word 'magic'. A famous magus called Zarathustra, unusually, worshipped a single god: Ahuru Mazda. His god's evil enemy was Angra Mainyu.

Weapons of war

- **Early stone axes and spears** may have been used both for hunting and as weapons. Remains of a half-a-million year-old wooden spear were found at Boxgrove, England.

- **A spear-thrower** was a stick with a notch in one end to take the end of a spear. With it, hunters (or fighters) could hurl a spear with tremendous force. Spear-throwers were the first ever machines made by humans, c.35,000BC.

▼ *The chariot was the airforce of the ancient civilizations, speeding archers and spear-throwers across the battlefield. Egyptians, Hittites and Assyrians fought huge battles with thousands of chariots.*

- **The first pictures** of bows come from North Africa, c.15,000-30,000BC. Bows could be devastatingly effective and were the main weapons of the earliest civilizations.

- **The invention** of bronze, c.3000BC, meant people could make metal swords, daggers, axes and spears.

- **A tiny bronze statue** of a chariot found at Tell Agrab, Iraq, dates from 3000BC. This is the first image of a chariot.

- **The Persian emperor** Cyrus (559-529BC) added scythes (long, sharp blades) poking out from chariot wheels to slice through the legs of enemy soldiers and horses.

- **The oldest helmet** (c.2500BC), made of a gold and silver alloy called electrum, was found in the royal tombs of Ur.

- **The crossbow** was invented in the Greek colony of Syracuse, about 400BC.

- **Alexander the Great** used giant crossbows firing 5 m arrows to win his empire between 340 and 323BC.

- **Around AD100,** Dionysius of Alexander in Egypt invented a rapid-firing crossbow, able to fire dozens of bolts a minute.

Tutankhamun

- **Tutankhamun** was pharaoh (king) of Ancient Egypt from 1347 to 1339BC. He was a boy when he became pharaoh and only 18 when he died.

- **Tutankhamun** was the last of the great 18th dynasty (family) of pharaohs who ruled Egypt 1567-1339BC. They included the warrior queen Hatshepsut, and Thutmose III, who led Egypt to the peak of its power around 1400BC.

- **Tutankhamun** was the son of Akhenaten, who with his queen Nefertiti created a revolution in Egypt. Akhenaten replaced worship of the old Egyptian gods with worship of a single god, and moved the capital to Armarna.

- **Tutankhamun's wife** was his half-sister Ankhesenamun. When he died – perhaps murdered – Ankhesenamun was at the mercy of his enemies, Ay and general Horemheb. She wrote to the Hittite king asking for his son to marry, but the Hittite prince was murdered on the way to Egypt. Ankhesenamun was forced to marry Ay, who thus became pharaoh. She also died young.

★ **STAR FACT** ★
Tutankhamun's third, inner coffin was made of over a tonne of solid gold.

- **The Valley of the Kings** near Luxor on the Nile in Egypt is the world's greatest archaeological site. It was the special burial place of the 18th dynasty pharaohs and contains the tombs of 62 pharaohs, and high officials.

- **Tutankhamun's** tomb was the only tomb in the Valley of the Kings not plundered over the centuries. When opened, it contained 5,000 items, including many fabulous carved and gold items.

- **Tutankhamun's** tomb was discovered by the English archaeologist Howard Carter, in 1922.

- **Rumours of a curse** on those disturbing the tomb began when Carter's pet canary was eaten by a cobra – the pharaoh's symbol – at the moment the tomb was opened.

- **Experts** worked out the dates of Tutankhamun's reign from the date labels on wine-jars left in the tomb.

◀ A fabulous gold mask was found in the innermost coffin, over the badly mummified remains of the young king. The skull showed signs of a fracture from a hammer.

In the burial chamber were four shrines of gilded wood, one inside the other

Inside the shrines, there was a red sandstone sarcophagus (coffin)

Inside the sarcophagus, there were three gold coffins, one inside the other

Beyond the burial chamber was a treasury full of gold and other treasures

Fabulous beds, chests, gold chariot wheels, and carved animals in the anteroom were just a taste of the riches to come

▶ When Carter opened Tutankhamun's tomb, he came first to an anteroom. It took him three years to clear this room and enter the burial chamber, with its huge gold shrines containing the coffins.

The Trojan Wars

- **From 1600 to 1100BC,** mainland Greece was dominated by tough warrior people called the Mycenaeans.

- **The Mycenaeans** fought with long bronze swords, long leather shields and bronze armour.

- **Mycenaeans** lived in small kingdoms, each with its own fortified hilltop city or *acropolis*.

- **A typical Mycenaean noble** was like a Viking chieftain. In the middle of his palace was a great hall with a central fireplace where warriors would sit around telling tales of heroic deeds.

- **After 1500BC** Mycenaean kings were buried in a beehive-shaped tomb called a *tholos*, with a long, corridor-shaped entrance.

▶ *Troy fell when the Greeks pretended to give up and go home, leaving behind a huge wooden horse. The jubilant Trojans dragged this into the city – only to discover Greeks hiding inside it.*

- **The Greek poet Homer** tells how a city called Troy was destroyed by the Mycenaeans after a ten-year siege. Historians once thought this was just a story, but now the remains of Troy have been discovered, they think there may be some truth in it.

- **The Trojan War** in Homer's tale is caused by the beautiful Helen of Sparta. She married Menalaus, brother of King Agamemnon of Mycenae, but she fell in love with Prince Paris of Troy.

- **Helen and Paris** eloped to Troy and Agamemnon and other Greeks laid siege to Troy to take her back.

- **The battle** featured many heroes – such as Hector, Achilles and Odysseus.

- **The Greeks** finally captured Troy when Greek soldiers hidden inside a wooden horse found their way into the city.

Early Greece

- **Around 1200BC,** the Mycenaeans began to abandon their cities, and a people called the Dorians took over Greece.

- **Many Mycenaeans** fled overseas in a large battle fleet, and the Egyptians called them the Sea Peoples. Some ended up in Italy and may have been the ancestors of the Etruscan people there.

- **With the end** of Mycenaean civilization, Greece entered the Dark Ages as the art of writing was lost.

- **About 800BC,** the Greeks began to emerge from the Dark Ages as they re-learned writing from the Phoenicians, a people who traded in the eastern Mediterranean.

- **The period** of Greek history from 800 to 500BC is called the Archaic (Ancient) Period.

- **In the Archaic Period,** the Greek population grew rapidly. States were governed by a few rich aristocrats.

- **The early Greeks** loved athletics and held four major events. They were called the Panhellenic Games and drew competitors from all over the Greek world.

- **The four Panhellenic Games** were the Olympic, Pythian, Isthmian and Nemean Games.

- **The Olympic Games** started in 776BC and were the most important. They were held every four years at Olympia.

- **The Greek poet Homer** wrote his famous poems about the Trojan Wars around 700BC.

◀ *A Greek house may have looked something like this 2,600 years ago, with first-floor bedrooms surrounding a courtyard.*

The Mayans

◀ The Mayan pyramid at Chichén Itzá in the Yucatán.

- **The Mayans** were a people who dominated Central America for 2,500 years until AD1441.

- **The Mayans** began building large pyramids with small temples on top between 600BC and AD250.

- **Mayan civilization** peaked between AD250 and 900. This is called the Classic Period.

- **During the Classic Period,** Mayan civilization centred on great cities such as Tikal in the Guatemalan lowlands. They traded far and wide on foot and in dug-out canoes.

> ★ STAR FACT ★
> The Mayans were brilliant astronomers and believed that the stars linked them to their gods.

- **Mayans in the Classic Period** developed a clever form of writing in symbols representing sounds or ideas. They recorded their history on stone monuments called *stelae*.

- **Mysteriously,** around AD800, the Mayans stopped making *stelae* and the Guatemalan cities were abandoned.

- **From AD800 to 1200,** the most powerful Mayan city was Chichén Itzá in the Yucatán region. From 1200 to 1440 another city, Mayapan, came to the fore. After 1440, Mayan civilization rapidly broke up, though no-one knows why.

- **The Mayans** were deeply religious. Deer, dogs, turkeys and even humans were often sacrificed to the gods in the temples on top of the pyramids.

- **Mayan farmers** grew mainly corn, beans and squash. From the corn, women made flat pancakes now called tortillas, and an alcoholic drink called *balche*.

Confucius

- **Confucius** is the most famous thinker and teacher in Chinese history.

- **Confucius** is the name used by Europeans. Chinese people called him Kongzi or K'ung-Fu-Tzu.

- **Confucius was born** in Lu, now Shantung Province, in 551BC, traditionally on 28 September, and died in 479BC.

- **Confucius mastered** the six Chinese arts – ritual, music, archery, charioteering, calligraphy (writing) and arithmetic – and became a brilliant teacher.

- **Confucius** was the first person in China to argue that all men should be educated to make the world a better place, and that teaching could be a way of life.

- **In middle age,** Confucius served as a minister for the King of Lu. He had a highly moral approach to public service. He told statesmen this golden rule: 'Do not do to others what you would not have them do to you.'

- **The King of Lu** was not interested in Confucius's ideas, so Confucius went into exile, followed by his students.

- **After his death,** Confucius's ideas were developed by teachers like Mencius (390-305BC) and Xunzi (c.250BC) into a way of life called Confucianism. Until recently, this dominated Chinese life.

- **Living at the same** time as Confucius may have been a man called Lao-Tse. Lao-Tse wrote the *Tao Te Ching*, the basis of Taoist religion.

- **The *Tao Te Ching*** tells of the *Tao* (Way) – the underlying unity of nature that makes everything what it is.

▶ Confucius's belief was that court officials should not plot for power but study music, poetry and the history of their ancestors.

Chinese technology

- **Western experts** have only recently realized that ancient Chinese technology was very advanced, and many of their early inventions only reached Europe thousands of years later.

- **In the early 1600s,** the great English thinker Francis Bacon said that three quite recent inventions had changed the world – printing, gunpowder and the ship's magnetic compass. All of these had been invented in China a thousand or more years earlier.

- **One of the oldest surviving** printed books is the *Diamond Sutra*, printed in China about AD868. But printing in China goes back to at least the 7th century AD.

▲ One particularly nasty Chinese invention was the 'Heaven-Rumbling Thunderclap Fierce Fire Erupter'. This was a gunpowder-fired device that shot out shells of poisonous gas.

▶ The Chinese made a magnetic compass called a sinan over 2,000 years ago. A ladle made of a magnetic stone called lodestone spins round on a shiny bronze plate to point south.

- **The world's first robot** was an amazing ancient Chinese cart with gears from the wheels that turned a statue on top so that its finger always pointed south.

- **The Chinese** had alcoholic spirits 2,000 years ago, over a thousand years before they came to Europe.

- **The horse stirrup** was invented in China in the 3rd century BC. This gave horse-soldiers a steady platform to fight from and allowed them to wear heavy armour.

- **The wheelbarrow** was invented by the Chinese c.100BC.

- **Cast-iron ploughs** were made in China around 200BC.

- **Football** was invented in China. About 200BC, they were playing a game called *t'su chu*. It involved kicking an inflated leather ball through a hole in a silk net.

▶ The Chinese discovered gunpowder and made the first guns about 1,100 years ago. They also became famous for their fireworks.

▲ Acupuncture involves sticking pins in certain points on the body to treat illness. The Chinese used it 1,800 years ago – but it may have been used earlier in Europe.

◀ The Chinese invented mechanical clocks in AD723 – 600 years earlier than Europe. This is Su Sung's 'Cosmic Engine', an amazing 10-m-high clock built at Khaifeng in AD1090.

◀ In AD132, Chang Heng made the world's first earthquake detector with a special jar. When even a faint, distant quake occurred, a metal ball would fall with a clang from the dragon's mouth at the top of the jar into the toad's mouth.

▶ Water-powered machines for spinning cloth are often thought of as inventions of the English Industrial Revolution in the 1700s. In fact, the Chinese were building them at least 500 years earlier, to spin a cloth called ramie.

The search for Troy

- **Troy is the city** in the Ancient Greek poet Homer's famous epic, the *Iliad*. It was once thought to be entirely mythical.

- **In 1822,** British scholar Charles McClaren suggested that Homer's Troy might be in Turkey. He pinpointed a mound called Hisarlik near the Dardanelles – a narrow sea linking the Black Sea and the Aegean.

- **German archaeologist** Heinrich Schliemann began digging at Hisarlik mound in 1871.

- **In 1873,** Schliemann uncovered fortifications and remains of a very ancient city, which he believed to be Troy.

- **Schliemann** also found a treasure of gold and silver which he called Priam's treasure after the Trojan King Priam mentioned in the *Iliad*. He smuggled this out of Turkey to take to Europe.

◀ When Schliemann found this gold mask at Mycenae, in 1876, he thought it must be Agamemnon's. In fact, it dates from 300 years earlier.

- **In 1876,** Schliemann was digging at Mycenae in Greece. He found what he thought was the tomb of Agamemnon, king of the Trojans' enemies in the *Iliad*.

- **In the 1890s,** Wilhelm Dorpfield showed that Hisarlik mound is made of nine layers of city remains. This is because the city was destroyed by fire or earthquake nine times. Each time the survivors built on the rubble.

- **Schliemann** thought Homer's Troy was Troy II (2), second layer from the bottom. Dorpfield thought it was Troy VI.

- **Troy I to V** (1 to 5) are now thought to date from the early Bronze Age (c.3000 to 1900BC).

- **Experts** now think Homer's Troy may be Troy VII, a layer of the seventh city, dating from about 1250BC.

Greek city-states

- **Ancient Greece** was not a single country in its early days, but a collection of independent cities or city-states.

- **A Greek city-state** was called a *polis* (plural *poleis*).

- *Polis* gives us the words politics and police – and polite.

- **There were several hundred** *poleis* in Ancient Greece. The largest were Athens and Sparta.

- **Each city** typically had a mound called an *acropolis* with a temple on top, and a market place called an *agora*.

> ★ **STAR FACT** ★
> The laws of the Athenian oligarch Draco were so harsh that severe laws are still called draconian.

- **To start with** (from about 800 to 600BC), city-states were governed by oligarchs (a few powerful men) or a tyrant, but people gradually got more say.

- **People in Greek city-states** were either free or slaves. Free men (not women) were split into citizens (born in the city itself) and *metics* (immigrants).

- **In 508BC,** a man called Cleisthenes gave Athens a new system of government called democracy.

- **Democracy** comes from the Greek word *demos* (people) and *kratos* (rule). The idea was that every citizen (but not metics and slaves) had the right to speak and vote in the Assembly, held every ten days on a hill called the Pnyx.

◀ The most famous acropolis is the Acropolis in Athens with the Parthenon temple on top, but nearly every polis had one.

Zhou and Qin dynasties

- **c.1100BC,** the Shang in China were conquered by a people called the Zhou.
- **The Zhou** extended the Shang's territory far across China, but the kingdom was divided into large estates, each with its own ruler.
- **In the time of the Zhou,** the Chinese began using iron, both for ploughs and weapons, and made many advances in technology.
- **Great thinkers** such as Laozi and Confucius came to the fore.
- **Confucius** believed morals were vital in government service, but a minister called Shang Yang (who died 338BC) thought the law must be strengthened by any means. This is called Legalism.
- **Shang Yang's** family – the Qin – overthrew the Zhou in 312BC.

▲ *Although today's brick and stone wall dates from the 1400s, the Great Wall of China was first built of earth bricks in 214BC, under Shi Huangdi.*

- **In 246BC,** Qin emperor Zheng expanded the empire and called himself Shi Huangdi, First Emperor. He had the 4,000-km-long Great Wall built to protect his empire from nomads from the north.
- **Shi Huangdi** banned books and buried 460 Confucian scholars alive. His eldest son Fu Su was banished when he objected.
- **When Shi Huangdi** died, in 210BC, his body was taken secretly to the capital by minister Li Si with a fish cart to hide the smell of rotting flesh. Li Si sent a letter to Fu Su, pretending it was from his father, telling him to commit suicide. Fu Su did and so Li Si came to power.
- **Shi Huangdi** was buried with an army of 6,000 life-size clay soldiers, called the Terracotta Army when found in 1974. Parts of the tomb are said to be booby-trapped.

Famous generals

▶ *Hannibal's greatest feat was leading an army – with elephants – through Spain and then the Alps in winter to attack Rome from the north.*

- **In 2300BC** King Sargon of Akkadia led his soldiers to victory over much larger armies by using especially far-shooting bows.
- **Tuthmose III** (1479-1425BC) was perhaps the greatest of the warrior pharaohs, fighting 17 campaigns and taking Egypt to its greatest extent.
- **Assurbanipal** (669-627BC) was the great Assyrian leader whose chariots gave him a powerful empire from the Nile to the Caucasus Mountains.
- **Sun-Tzu** was the Chinese military genius who, in 500BC, wrote the first manual on the art of war.
- **Alexander the Great** was the Macedonian whose army of

35,000 was the most efficient yet seen – and who perfected the phalanx.

- **Hannibal** (247-182BC) was the greatest general of the powerful city of Carthage (now near Tunis in Africa).
- **Scipio** (237-183BC) was the Roman general who conquered Spain and broke Carthaginian power in Africa.
- **Julius Caesar** was the greatest Roman general.
- **Belisarius** (AD505-565) and Narses (AD478-573) were generals for Byzantine Emperor Justinian. Their mounted archers defeated the Vandals and Goths.
- **Charles Martel** (AD688-741), 'the Hammer', was the Frankish king who defeated the Moors at Tours in France in AD732 and turned back the Arab conquest of Europe.

Buddha

- **Buddha** was the founder of the Buddhist religion, who lived in India c.563-483BC.

- **Buddha's** real name was Siddhartha Gautama.

- **Buddha** is not a name but a title (like the messiah) meaning 'enlightened one', so you should really say 'the Buddha'.

- **Archaeological excavations** finished in 1995 suggest that a man who may have been Siddhartha lived in the palace of his father Suddodhana on what is now the border of Nepal and India.

- **As a young prince,** Siddhartha lived a life of luxury. When he was 16 years old, he married his cousin the Princess Yasodhara, who was also 16 years old.

◀ *Most statues of the Buddha show him sitting cross-legged deeply meditating (thinking).*

- **The turning point** was when Siddhartha was 29 and he saw four visions: an old man, a sick man, a corpse and a wandering holy man.

- **The first three visions** told Siddhartha that life involved ageing, sickness and death. The fourth told him he must leave his wife and become a holy man.

- **After six years of** self-denial, Siddhartha sat down under a shady 'bo' tree to think – and after several hours the answer came to him.

- **The Buddha** spent the rest of his life preaching his message around India.

- **The Buddha** died at the age of 80. His bones became sacred relics.

Greek thinkers

◀ *Aristotle, the brilliant tutor to Alexander the Great, was thought of as the ultimate authority on every subject for over 2,000 years.*

- **The great thinkers** of Ancient Greece were called philosophers. Philosophy is Greek for 'love of wisdom'.

- **The key philosophers** were Socrates, Plato and Aristotle.

- **Socrates** (466-399BC) believed people would behave well if they knew what good behaviour was and challenged people to think about truth, good and evil.

- **Plato** (427-348BC) argued that, behind the messy chaos of everyday experience, there is a perfect and beautiful Idea or Form. He also tried to find the ideal way of governing a state.

- **Aristotle** (384-322BC) argued that, for true knowledge, you must find the 'final cause' – why something happens.

- **Aristotle** was the first great scientist, stressing the need to collect data, sort the results and interpret them.

- **Many of the basic** ideas in philosophy, even today, come from Socrates, Plato and Aristotle, and other Greek philosophers such as Epicurus and Diogenes.

- **Greek mathematicians** such as Euclid, Appolonius, Pythagoras and Archimedes worked out many of our basic rules of maths. Most school geometry still depends on the system devised by Euclid.

- **Greek astronomers** like Aristarchus and Anaxagoras made many brilliant deductions – but many of these were forgotten. Aristarchus realized that the Earth turned on its axis and circled the Sun. Yet it was almost 2,000 years before this idea was generally accepted.

> ★ STAR FACT ★
> Archimedes showed how the effect of a lever could be worked out by maths.

Homer

- **Homer** is the Ancient Greek poet said to have written the ancient world's two greatest poems: the *Iliad* and the *Odyssey*.

- **Homer probably** lived in the 9th century BC in Ionia, on what is now the Aegean coast of Turkey, or on the island of Chios.

- **No one knows** for certain if Homer existed, or if he composed all of both poems. Most experts think he did.

- **In Homer's time** there was a great tradition of bards. These were poets who recited aloud great tales of heroic deeds. They knew the poems by heart and so never wrote them down.

- **The *Iliad* and the *Odyssey*** are the only poems from the times of the bards that were written down and so survive. They may have been written down at the time, or later.

- **After Homer's time** the two great poems were used in religious festivals in Greece.

◀ Nothing is known for certain about Homer, but legend says he was blind.

- **For centuries** after Homer's time, Greek children learned to read, and learned about the legends of the past, by studying Homer's two great poems.

- **In the 2nd century BC,** scholars at the Alexandrian Library in Egypt studied the poems. A few scholars came to the conclusion that they were so different in style they must have been written by two different poets.

- **The *Iliad*** is a long poem in lofty language about the Trojan Wars, in which the Greeks besiege the city of Troy to take back the kidnapped Helen.

- **The *Odyssey*** tells the amazing adventures of hero Odysseus on a great journey.

Early Americans

▲ Carving wooden duck decoys for hunting is a North American tradition dating back thousands of years.

- **The Americas** were the last continents humans occupied.

- **The first Americans** may have been Australian aboriginals who arrived by boat 50,000 years ago.

- **Ancestors of today's Native Americans** probably came to the Americas 20-35,000 years ago, from Asia. They are thought to have walked across the strip of land that once joined Asia and North America across the Bering Strait.

! NEWS FLASH !
A 50,000 year-old skull found in Colombia resembles the skulls of Australian aboriginals.

- **By 6000BC, the first Native Americans** had spread south from Alaska and far down into South America.

- **There is evidence** that humans were living in Mexico over 20,000 years ago. At El Jobo in Colombia, pendants dating back to 14,920BC have been found.

- **10,000 years ago,** groups of 'Paleo-Indians' on North America's Great Plains hunted now-extinct animals such as camels and mammoths. In the dry western mountains, Desert peoples planted wild grass-seed.

- **In Mexico,** people began to grow squash, peppers and beans at least 8,500 years ago.

- **Corn was probably first** grown around 7,000 years ago.

- **Corn, beans and squash** provided food for early American civilizations such as the Olmecs and Mayans.

Greek art

A chorus linked the scenes with verse and songs

The circular acting area was called the orchestra

A typical theatre, like the Theatre of Dionysus in Athens, seated 14,000 in stadium-like rows

Scenes were played by just two or three actors, each wearing a mask

Audiences took cushions to sit on and picnics to keep them going

Behind the orchestra was a house or 'skene' where the actors changed. Later this became a backdrop.

▶ Formal drama was developed in Ancient Greece in the 5th and 6th centuries BC. Huge audiences watched plays in open-air arenas.

In later Greek theatres, the skene developed side wings here called paraskinia

- **In the heyday of Ancient Greece,** thousands of sculptors, architects, painters, dramatists and poets were creating a fantastic wealth of beautiful works of art.

- **The Greeks** made graceful statues and friezes to decorate temples and homes. They were carved mostly from marble and limestone and then painted, though in surviving statues the paint has worn away.

- **The most famous sculptors** were Phidias (c.490-420BC), Praxiteles (c.330BC), Lysippus (c.380-306BC) and Myron (c.500-440BC). Phidias's huge gold and ivory statue of the god Zeus was famous throughout the ancient world.

- **Greek architects** such as Ictinus and Callicrates created beautiful marble and limestone temples fronted by graceful columns and elegant triangular friezes. The most famous is the Parthenon in Athens.

- **The Greeks** had three styles for columns: the simple Doric, the slender Ionic, topped by scrolls, and the ornate Corinthian, topped by sculpted acanthus leaves.

- **The style** created by the Greek temples is now called Classical and has influenced architects ever since.

- **The Greeks** believed each art was inspired by one of nine goddesses called Muses.

- **Ancient Greek writers** include the poets Homer, Sappho and Pindar. They created styles of writing including epic poetry.

- **The tragedy** is a grand drama doomed to end unhappily for the hero. Tragedy was created by Greek dramatists such as Aeschylus, Euripides and Sophocles, who wrote the tragedy King Oedipus.

> ★ STAR FACT ★
> The Colossus of Rhodes was a huge 37-m-high statue cast in bronze by Greek sculptor Chares. It stood near to the harbour of Rhodes, an island in the Aegean Sea.

▶ The famous Venus de Milo was found on the Aegean island of Milos in AD 1820. It was carved in Greek Antioch (now in Turkey) around 150BC and shows the goddess of love Aphrodite (Roman goddess Venus). The statue originally had arms.

What people ate

- **1.5 million years ago,** people learned how to use fire to cook food. The oldest known cooking fire is at Swartkrans, South Africa.

- **The first ovens** were pits for hot coals, first used in the Ukraine about 20,000 years ago. The first real ovens were from Sumer and Egypt, c.2600BC.

- **Grain seeds** were cooked and mixed with water to make gruel (porridge). c.20,000 years ago, people learned to bake gruel on a hot stone to make flat bread, like pitta.

- **Pottery** meant liquids could be heated to make stews. The oldest pottery is 13,000-year-old pots from Odai-Yamomoto in Japan. The first pots from the Near East, from Iran, date back 11,000 years.

- **c.12,000 years ago,** people found how to make food last by letting it ferment, making cheese from milk and wine from grapes.

▶ *The earliest people simply ate what food they could find — either by hunting (like fish) or gathering (like berries).*

◀ *Bread was the first processed food, made by baking ground-up grass seeds mixed with water.*

- **c.8000BC,** people began to farm animals such as sheep and grow plants such as cereals for food. Diets became less varied than when people gathered food wild, but much more reliable.

- **c.4000BC** special farmers in Palestine were growing oil-rich olives to squeeze and make olive oil in huge amounts. Romans consumed vast quantities.

- **c.2600BC,** the Egyptians found that, by leaving gruel to ferment, they could make a dough. This they baked in ovens to make the first raised bread.

- **Honey** was the main sweetener. Egyptians kept bees for honey and also made sweet syrups from fruits.

- **The oldest recipe book** is an Assyrian stone tablet from 1700BC with 25 recipes, including a bird called a *tarru* cooked in onion, garlic, milk and spices.

The Phoenicians

- **From about 3000BC,** Semitic peoples such as Canaanites lived on the eastern Mediterranean coast and built the great city of Byblos.

- **From about 1100BC,** the people living here became known as Phoenicians.

- **The word 'phoenicians'** comes from *phoinix*, the Greek word for a purple dye made famous by these people.

▶ *Phoenicians were master seafarers. Broad merchant ships called gaulos carried goods. Fifty-oared rowing galleys like this defended the ports from attack.*

Hull built from the famed cedars of Lebanon trees

- **The Phoenicians** were great sea traders. Their ports, of Tyre and Sidon bustled with ships carrying goods from all over the known world.

- **The Phoenicians** used wool from Mesopotamia and flax and linen from Egypt to make cloth. They also made jewellery from imported gems, metals and ivory.

- **Phoenicians** invented the alphabet and gave us the word too. The Phoenician words *aleph* ('ox') and *beth* ('house') became the Greek letters *alpha* and *beta*. The word Bible and the prefix *bibli-* (meaning 'books') come from Byblos.

- **The dye** for which the Phoenicians were famous was made from the shells of murex snails.

- **c.600BC,** Phoenician sailors sailed from the Red Sea right round Africa and back into the Mediterranean.

- **Phoenicians** set up colonies across the Mediterranean as far west as Gades (now Cadiz, in Spain).

- **The greatest** Phoenician colony was the city of Carthage in what is now Tunisia.

Polynesians

- **Polynesians** are the people who live on the islands in the middle of the Pacific Ocean, from Hawaii to Easter Island and New Zealand.

- **There are 10,000** islands in Polynesia and the rest of the eastern Pacific, with hundreds of different cultures and languages, each with its own history.

- **Many Polynesian islands** may well have been first settled 40,000 years ago by people from Southeast Asia.

- **2,000 years ago,** a second wave of migrants moved east from Fiji, Samoa and Tonga to the Marquesas Islands.

- **The settlers** crossed the ocean in small double canoes and outriggers.

- **In their canoes** the settlers took crops (coconuts, yams, taros and breadfruit) and livestock (pigs and chickens).

> ★ STAR FACT ★
> The biggest *moai* statues on Easter Island are up to 12 m tall and weigh 90 tonnes.

▲ There are about 600 huge stone *moai* statues on Easter Island, on platforms called ahus. No one knows what they were for.

- **Every island** developed its own style of woodcarving.

- **About AD400,** the new Polynesians moved on to Hawaii and Easter Island.

- **Easter Islanders** created strange stone statues called *moais*, carved with stone tools since they had no metal.

Greek gods and myths

- **The Greeks** had a wealth of myths – stories about their gods, goddesses, heroes and villains.

- **We know** about the myths mainly from Homer's poems and Hesiod's book *Theogeny*, both from about 700BC.

- *Theogeny* tells how the Earth began, with the earth goddess Gaia emerging from chaos and giving birth to Uranus, the king of the sky.

- **The many children** of Gaia and Uranus were called the Titans, led by Cronos.

- **Cronos** married his sister Rhea. Their children, led by Zeus, rebelled against the Titans to become the new top gods, called the Olympians.

- **The Olympians** were said to live on Mt Olympus, and include the most famous Greek gods, such as Apollo the god of light, Demeter the goddess of crops, Artemis the goddess of the Moon and Dionysius the wine god.

- **Greek heroes** were mostly heroes from the times of the Trojan Wars or earlier.

- **Early heroes** include Jason, who led his Argonauts (his crew) in search of the fabulous Golden Fleece, and Theseus, who killed the minotaur.

- **Trojan war heroes** included Achilles and Odysseus.

- **The greatest hero** was super-strong Heracles, whom the Romans later called Hercules.

◄ The Romans adopted many Greek gods. These are Venus (Greek goddess Aphrodite), the goddess of love, and Mercury (Hermes) the winged foot-messenger.

Alexander the Great

▶ In just nine years and a series of brilliant campaigns, Alexander created a vast empire. No one knows exactly what his plans were. However, the teachings of his tutor Aristotle were important to him, and he had his own vision of different peoples living together in friendship.

Alexander's route

● **Alexander the Great** was a young Macedonian king who was one of the greatest generals in history. He built an empire stretching from Greece to India.

● **Alexander** was born in 356BC in Pella, capital of Macedonia. His father King Phillip II was a tough fighter who conquered neighbouring Greece. His mother was the fiery Olympias, who told him that he was descended from Achilles, the hero of the *Iliad*.

● **As a boy,** he was tutored by the famous philosopher Aristotle. A story tells how he tamed the great unridable horse Bucephalus, which afterwards carried him as far as India.

● **When Alexander was 20,** his father was murdered by a bodyguard and he became king. Alexander quickly stamped out rebellion.

▶ The key to Macedonian success was the phalanx. In a phalanx, armoured soldiers stood in tightly packed rows bristling with long spears. Such a formation could withstand a cavalry attack, yet still move swiftly.

> ★ STAR FACT ★
> An old legend said that anyone who untied a tricky knot in a town called Gordium would conquer Asia. Alexander instantly sliced through this Gordian knot with his sword.

● **In 334BC,** Alexander crossed the narrow neck of sea separating Europe from Asia with his army. Within a year, he had conquered the mighty Persian Empire.

● **In 331BC,** Alexander led his army on into Egypt where he was made pharaoh and founded the city of Alexandria. He trekked on to the desert oasis of Siwah where legend says an oracle proclaimed him son of the god Zeus.

● **In 327BC,** he married the lovely Bactrian princess, Roxane.

● **After capturing** the city of Babylon and finishing off Persian King Darius, Alexander led his conquering army into India. Here his homesick troops finally asked to go home.

● **In 325BC, Alexander had** ships built and carried his army down the Indus River and returned to Babylon. Within a year, he fell ill and died.

The founding of Rome

- **People lived** in Italy long before Rome was founded and a people called the Etruscans created an advanced civilization in the northwest between 800 and 400BC.

- **According to legend,** Rome was founded in 753BC by the twins Romulus and Remus, who were said to have been brought up by a she-wolf.

- **By 550BC,** Rome was a big city ruled by Etruscan kings.

- **In 509BC,** the Roman people drove out the kings and made themselves an independent republic.

- **Republican Rome** was ruled by the Senate, an assembly made up of 100 patricians (men from leading families).

- **In theory,** Rome was governed by the people. But real power was in the hands of patricians; plebeians (ordinary citizens) had little. Slaves had no power or rights at all.

- **Plebeians** fought for power and, by 287BC, gained the right to stand as consuls, the highest official posts.

- **In the 400s** and 300s BC, Rome extended its power all over Italy by brute force and alliances.

▲ *Legend has it that Rome was founded by the twins Romulus and Remus, who were brought up by a she-wolf.*

- **By 264BC,** Rome rivalled Carthage, the North African city that dominated the western Mediterranean. In 164BC, Rome destroyed Carthage totally after the Punic Wars.

- **By 130BC** Rome had built a mighty empire stretching from Spain to Turkey and along the North African coast.

Cleopatra

- **Cleopatra** (69-30BC) was the last Macedonian queen of Egypt. She was descended from Ptolemy, a general of Alexander the Great who made himself king after Alexander died.

- **Cleopatra may** have been beautiful. She was certainly intelligent, charming and highly determined.

- **Cleopatra** became queen in 51BC, when her father died. Her ten-year-old brother Ptolemy became king.

- **Ptolemy's guardians** seized power and drove Cleopatra out. She was restored to the throne by the Roman armies of Julius Caesar.

- **Legend has it** that Cleopatra had herself delivered to Caesar rolled up in a carpet. Whatever the truth, he fell in love with her, and she had a son, Caesarion, by him.

- **Caesar** invited Cleopatra and Caesarion to Rome, where she stayed until 44BC, when Caesar was assassinated.

◄ *Octavian described Cleopatra as a wicked temptress and the idea has stuck. But her people in Egypt thought of her as a great, just and much-loved queen.*

- **The Roman general** Mark Antony went to Cleopatra for her support in his bid for power in Rome. He too fell in love with her. They later married and had three children.

- **Mark Antony** returned to Rome to make a political marriage to Octavia, sister of Octavian. But he soon returned to Cleopatra.

- **Mark Antony and Cleopatra** were ambitious and strove to take over the eastern Roman Empire. But their armies were defeated at the Battle of Actium, off Greece, in 31BC by the forces of Octavian (later Augustus Caesar).

- **As Octavian** chased them to Alexandria, Cleopatra spread rumours that she was dead. In despair, Mark Antony stabbed himself. He died in her arms. Cleopatra tried to make peace with Octavian but failed. She took her life by placing an asp, a poisonous snake, on her breast.

The rise of Rome

- **As Rome's** empire spread, the creation of plantations worked by slaves put small farmers out of work. The gap between rich and poor widened.

- **Many joined** the army to escape poverty and became more loyal to their generals than to the Senate.

- **Two popular generals,** Pompey and Julius Caesar, used their armies to take over Rome and suspend the Republic.

- **Caesar and Pompey** argued, and after battles right across the empire, Caesar gained the upper hand.

◄ Many Romans lived in comfortable two-storey townhouses (domi), with heated pools and underfloor heating.

- **Once in power,** Caesar restored order and passed laws to reduce people's debts.

- **Caesar** was made dictator and ruled Rome without the Senate.

- **In 44BC,** a man called Brutus killed Caesar to restore the Republic – but Caesar's place was taken by another general, Octavian, Caesar's adopted son.

- **By 27BC,** Octavian was so powerful he declared himself the first Roman Emperor and took the name Augustus.

- **Under Augustus,** rebellious parts of Spain and the Alps were brought under control and the empire was expanded along the Rhine and Danube Rivers.

- **By 1BC,** the days of strife were over and Rome presided over a vast, stable, prosperous empire.

Jesus

- **Jesus Christ** was one of the world's great religious leaders. The religion of Christianity is based on his teachings.

- **Our knowledge** of Jesus's life comes almost entirely from four short books in the Bible's New Testament: the gospels of Matthew, Mark, Luke and John.

- **Roman writers** such as Pliny mention Jesus briefly.

- **Jesus** was born in Bethlehem in Palestine between 4 and 1BC.

◄ Jesus is his own name. Christ is a title that comes from the Greek word christos, which means 'anointed one'.

- **The Bible** tells how his poor young virgin mother Mary became miraculously pregnant after a visit by the archangel Gabriel, and that Jesus is the only Son of God.

- **Little** is known of Jesus's childhood. His teaching began after he was baptized by John the Baptist at the age of 30.

- **Jesus's mission** was to announce that the Kingdom of God was coming. From his many followers, he chose 12 'apostles' to help him spread the word.

- **Jesus performed** all kinds of miracles to convince people of the truth of his teachings.

- **Many Jews** felt Jesus was a troublemaker, especially after a triumphal entry into Jerusalem. They had the Roman governor Pontius Pilate put him to death by crucifixion (nailing to a cross).

★ STAR FACT ★
After his death, Jesus was said to have been resurrected – brought to life again.

The Han dynasty

- **In 210BC,** the small Han kingdom was ruled over by Liu Bang. Liu Bang was a poor villager who had come to power as the Qin Empire broke down.

- **In 206BC,** Liu Bang led an army on the Qin capital, Xiangyang. He looted Shi Huangdi's tomb, and burned the city and the library containing the books Shi Huangdi had banned – the only existing copies.

- **In 202BC,** Liu Bang proclaimed himself first Han emperor and took the name Gaozu.

- **Under the Han,** China became as large and powerful as the Roman Empire, and art and science thrived. Chinese people still sometimes call themselves Han.

- **Under Wudi** (141–87BC), Han China reached its peak.

- **Han cities** were huge, crowded and beautiful, and craftsmen made many exquisite things from wood, paint and silk – sadly destroyed when Han rule ended.

- **Silk, jade and horses** were traded along the Silk Route, through Asia as far as the Roman Empire.

▶ Beautiful objects like this bronze urn were traded between China and Europe along the famous Silk Route for thousands of years.

- **Han emperors** tried to recover the lost writings and revived the teachings of Confucius. Public officials became scholars and in 165BC the first exams for entry into public service were held.

- **About AD50,** Buddhist missionaries reached China.

- **By AD200,** the Han emperors were weakened by their ambitious wives and eunuchs (guardians). Rebellions by a group called the Yellow Turbans, combined with attacks by warriors from the north, brought the empire down.

Roman towns

- **Roman towns** were the biggest and most sophisticated the world had seen. They were not built on rigid grids like Greek cities, but they all had common features.

- **Roman towns** had two main streets and many side streets with spaces in between called *insulae* (islands).

- **The *insulae*** were tightly packed with private houses – houses of the rich called *domi* and apartment blocks (also called *insulae*). The bigger houses had courtyards.

- **Traffic jams** were so common that many towns banned wheeled traffic from the streets during daylight.

- **Most towns** had numerous shops, inns (*tabernae*), cafés (*thermopilia*) and bakeries (*pistrina*).

- **The forum** was a large open market and meeting place surrounded on three sides by a covered walkway. The fourth side was the law courts and town hall (*basilica*).

- **Most towns** had many grand temples to Roman gods.

- **Most towns** had a large open-air theatre. There was also a games arena or stadium where warriors called gladiators fought and chariot races were held.

- **The bath houses** (*thermae*) were places where people came to sit around and dip into hot and cold baths in magnificent surroundings.

- **Towns** had very good water supplies and sewage systems.

◀ The remains of the forum in Rome give a glimpse of just how magnificent Roman cities must have been.

The Roman Empire

Gladiators were prisoners and criminals who were made to fight in big arenas called amphitheatres to entertain people.

◀ This map shows the empire at its peak under the Emperor Trajan (AD98-117). It was divided into areas called provinces, such as Britannia (England and Wales) and Gallia (northern France). Each had its own Roman governor, often a retired consul (minister), who used his power to extort taxes.

- **For 200 years** after Augustus became emperor in 27BC, Roman emperors ruled over an empire so large and secure that citizens could talk of the *Pax Romana* (Roman Peace).

- **The Romans** built straight roads to move their troops about quickly. On the whole, they governed peacefully and also built hundreds of towns in the Roman manner.

- **After Augustus** died, in AD14, his stepson Tiberius succeeded him. Then came a succession of Augustus's descendants, including Gaius, Claudius and Nero.

- **Gaius** (AD37-41) was known as Caligula ('little boots') because of the soldiers' boots he wore as a child.

- **Soon after** Caligula became emperor, an illness left him mad. He spent wildly, had people whipped and killed, married and murdered his sister and elected his horse as a minister. Eventually he was murdered by soldiers.

- **Claudius** (AD41-54) replaced Caligula. People thought he was stupid because he stuttered and was crippled. But he proved the wisest and most humane of all emperors.

- **Claudius** was probably poisoned by his 4th wife Agrippina, who wanted power for her son Nero.

- **The power of Roman emperors** reached a peak under the 'Antonines' – Nerva, Trajan, Hadrian, Antoninus and Marcus Aurelius. They ruled AD96-180.

- **The empire** grew only a little after Augustus. Britain was conquered in AD43, and Trajan took Dacia (now Hungary and Romania).

★ STAR FACT ★
Roman historian Suetonius claimed Nero sang and played the lyre during Rome's great fire in AD64.

▶ Leading imperial officials wore distinctive flowing robes called togas, with a strip dyed in a rare purple called Tyrian purple. Laws were written on papyrus or parchment.

The Roman army

- **Rome owed its power** to its highly efficient army.
- **In a crisis,** Rome could raise an army of 800,000 men.
- **The Roman army** fought mainly on foot, advancing in tight squares bristling with spears and protected by large shields called *scutari*. They often put shields over their heads to protect them from arrows. This formation was called a *testudo* or tortoise.
- **Under the Republic,** the army was divided into legions of 5,000 soldiers. Legions were made of 10 cohorts. Cohorts were made of centuries of 80-100 soldiers.
- **Each legion** was led by a *legatus*. A cohort was led by a *tribunus militum*. A century was led by a centurion.
- **All Roman soldiers** had a short sword (60 cm long) and carried two throwing spears. They also wore armour – first, vests of chain mail and a leather helmet; later, metal strips on a leather tunic and a metal helmet.
- **Roman armies** built huge siege engines and catapults called *ballistas* when they had to capture a town.
- **After 100BC,** most soldiers were professionals, who joined the army for life. Food took about a third of their wages.
- **In training,** soldiers went on forced 30 km marches three times a month. They moved at 8 km per hour, carrying very heavy packs.
- **Soldiers** were flogged for misbehaviour. Mutiny was punished by executing one in ten suspects. This was called decimation.

▶ The tough Roman soldier marched carrying all his weapons and armour, plus a heavy pack full of clothes, food and tools for digging and building.

The Roman way of life

- **In big cities,** rich Romans had a comfortable way of life.
- **For breakfast,** Romans typically ate bread or wheat biscuits with honey, dates or olives, and water or wine.
- **A Roman lunch** (*prandium*) consisted of much the same things as breakfast.
- **Romans had** *cena* (the main meal) in the afternoon, after a visit to the baths. This became a very lavish affair with three main courses, each with many dishes.

> ★ STAR FACT ★
> The Circus Maximus chariot racetrack in Rome held up to 250,000 spectators.

- **Rich Romans** had a lot of free time, since slaves did all the work. Leisure activities included gambling by tossing coins (*capita et navia*) and knucklebones (*tali*).
- **Public entertainments** were called *ludi* (games). They included theatre, chariot races, and fights with gladiators (trained fighters) and animals.
- **The Emperor Trajan** went to a gladiator contest that lasted 117 days and involved 10,000 gladiators.
- **Romans** had more slaves than any empire in history. Many were treated cruelly, but some lived quite well.
- **In 90BC,** a man called Spartacus led a revolt of slaves that lasted two years, until crushed by Roman armies.

◀ Romans were very clean and often went to the public baths or bathed at home. These are the Roman baths at Bath, England.

Famous disasters

▲ The Greek island of Santorini was blown apart in 1500BC by a giant volcanic eruption, so ending the Minoan civilization.

- **Many ancient civilizations** had legends of great floods.

- **In the Middle East,** a Sumerian named Ziusudra, the Babylonian Gilgamesh and the Jewish Noah all built an ark (boat) to ride out a flood that drowned all others.

- **In India,** Manu, the first man and first king, was warned by fish and survived the great flood by building a boat.

- **In the Americas,** the Aztecs believed four previous worlds had been destroyed by jaguars, hurricanes, thunder and lightning and a huge 52-year flood.

- **The huge eruption** of the Aegean island volcano of Thera (Santorini), in 1500BC, effectively destroyed Minoan civilization on Crete – and may have started legends of the lost civilization of Atlantis, drowned by a tidal wave.

- **While the Jews** were slaves there, Egypt was ruined by a flood of blood predicted by the Jew Moses – now thought to have been the Nile River in flood, stained by red algae.

- **In 464BC,** 10,000 were killed by an earthquake that rocked the Greek city of Sparta.

- **In 436BC,** a famine drove thousands of Romans to jump into the Tiber River to escape the pain of starvation.

- **In AD64,** the Rome of Emperor Nero was destroyed by a great fire. Angry people said that Nero had started it.

- **In AD79,** the Roman city of Pompeii was buried under ash from nearby volcano Vesuvius – and preserved to this day.

Yamato

- **The oldest signs** of farming in Japan date back to 300BC, but Japan was inhabited long before that.

  - **The first known inhabitants** of Japan were the Ainu or Ezo, who were short, hairy, fair-skinned people. Some Ainu people still survive in northern Japan.

    - **About 250BC,** the Yayoi tribe became dominant in Japan. They used iron and bronze.

◀ Shinto priests believe that all things that inspire awe – from twisted trees to dead warriors – have kami (spirits).

- **In AD167,** priestess Himiko unified Japan under her rule.

- **Himiko** sent ambassadors to China for support, and imported many Chinese ideas.

- **From AD200-645,** the Yamato tribe dominated Japan. The Yamato conquered Korea and were the first emperors.

- **Right up to today,** Japanese emperors claim to be descended from the Yamato, who, in turn, claimed to be descended from the Shinto sun-goddess, Amaterasu.

- **Shotoku Taishi** (AD574-622) was a young regent for old Empress Suiko. He gave Japan organized Chinese-style government and promoted Buddhism and Confucianism.

- **Shinto** or 'way of the gods' has been Japan's religion since prehistoric times. It got its name in the 6th century to distinguish it from Buddhism and Confucianism.

> **! NEWS FLASH !**
> In AD2000, the postholes of a round hut half a million years old were found in Japan.

The Mauryan Empire

- **In 321BC,** the first great Indian empire was created by Chandragupta Maurya (c.325-297BC). Its capital was Pataliputra on the Ganges.

- **The Mauryan Empire** at its peak included most of modern Pakistan, Bangladesh and India – except for the very southern tip.

- **The most famous** Mauryan emperor was Chandragupta's grandson Asoka (c.265-238BC).

- **After witnessing** a horrific battle, Asoka was so appalled by the suffering that he resolved never to go to war. He devoted himself to improving the lot of his people.

- **Asoka** became a Buddhist and his government promoted the *Dharma,* or 'Universal Law'.

▲ *During Asoka's reign, stupas (domed shrines) containing relics of the Buddha were built all over India.*

- **The Universal Law** preached religious tolerance, non-violence and respect for the dignity of every single person.

- **Asoka's men** dug wells and built reservoirs all over India to help the poor. They also provided comfortable rest-houses and planted shady banyan trees for travellers along the new roads.

- **Asoka said** 'all men are my children', and sent officials out to deal with local problems.

- **A vast secret police force** and an army of 700,000 helped Asoka to run his empire.

- **Asoka's** Sarnath lion insignia is now India's national emblem.

Early North Americans

- **Maize** was grown in southwestern USA c.2000-1000BC.

- **The first farming villages** in the southwest were those of the Anasazi, Mogollon and Hohokam peoples and dated from AD100. They lived either in caves or in underground 'pit houses' carved into the desert rock.

- **Anasazi** is Navajo Indian for 'Ancient Ones'.

- **The first Anasazi** are also known as Basket Makers because of their skill in weaving baskets.

- **About AD700,** the Anasazi began to build large stone villages called *pueblos,* which is why from this time they are also called Pueblo Indians.

- **In the 'Classic' Pueblo** period, from AD1050-1300, the Anasazi lived in huge apartments carved out of cliffs, like Pueblo Bonito. Pueblo culture began to fade c.AD1300.

▲ *The most famous cliff pueblos are in Mesa Verde, Colorado.*

- **In the east,** the first farming villages were those of the Hopewell peoples of the Illinois and Ohio valleys, between 100BC and AD200.

- **The Hopewell people** are known for their burial mounds. Things found in these mounds show they traded all over America.

- **About AD700,** farming villages with temple mounds developed near St Louis on the Mississippi.

> ★ STAR FACT ★
> Cliff Palace in Mesa Verde had space for 250 people in its 217 rooms.

Early Ireland

- **Ireland** was settled late. The first proof of settlers are 8,000-year-old flints left by hunters and fishers on beaches in the northeast, near the modern town Larne.

- **The New Stone Age** (Neolithic) began when the first farms and permanent homes appeared, 5,000 years ago.

- **Neolithic people** honoured their dead with long mounds or barrows – called 'court graves' because they have a courtyard at the entrance. They also built barrows called portal graves with three huge stones set like a door.

- **The most dramatic remains** from earliest times are 'passage' graves. Inside an earth mound a long passage leads to a stone chamber. Of 150 in Ireland, the most famous is Newgrange in the Boyne valley near Dublin.

- **The Celts** invaded Ireland in the Iron Age, about 400BC, and many of Ireland's rich collection of heroic myths are probably based in this time.

- **Celtic Ireland** was split into 150 kingdoms or clans called *tuatha* and later into five provinces – Ulster, Meath, Leinster, Munster and Connaught. After AD500, there was a high king (*ard-ri*) ruling Ireland from Tara in Leinster.

- **Irish Celts** were both warriors and herdsmen who valued cows highly. They also revered poets (*file*), and their metalwork, revealed in items such as the Tara brooch and the Ardagh chalice, is extraordinarily beautiful.

- **Early Celtic priests** were druids, but in AD432, St Patrick, legend says, came to convert Ireland to Christianity.

- **Irish monasteries** became havens of art and learning in the Dark Ages, creating the famous *Book of Kells*.

▼ *The huge burial mound at Newgrange was built around 3100BC. A long, narrow passage leads to a burial chamber deep inside the mound. Above the entrance is an unusual 'roof-box' – a special slot through which the midwinter sun shines into the chamber.*

Every year, at exactly 8.58 am on 21 December (the winter solstice), the rising sun shines through this roof-box and right down the passage to light up the burial chamber

One of Newgrange's most distinctive features is the rich ornamentation – especially the carved spirals, which must have had some ritual significance

Julius Caesar

- **Julius Caesar** (c.100-44BC) was Rome's most famous general and leader. He was also a great speaker who had the power to excite huge crowds.

- **Caesar's** individuality was clear from the start. At 17, he defied Sulla, the dictator of Rome and married Cornelia, the daughter of the rebel leader Cinna. Cornelia died when Caesar was about 30.

- **Caesar** began as a politician and made himself popular by spending his own money on public entertainments.

- **In 60BC,** he formed a powerful triumvirate (threesome) with Crassus and Pompey, which dominated Rome.

- **In 58BC,** Caesar led a brilliant campaign to conquer Gaul (now northern France), and invaded Britain.

- ◄ *Caesar was not only a brilliant general, but a great statesman who brought in many reforms and tried to stamp out corruption.*

- **Caesar** wrote an account of his campaigns in Gaul that is a classic of historical writing.

- **Pompey** was alarmed by the fame that Caesar's conquests brought him. The two began a war that lasted five years, ending in Egypt in 48BC, where Caesar met and fell in love with Cleopatra.

- **By 45BC,** Caesar was undisputed master of the Roman Empire. The people elected him dictator for life.

- **Caesar** was asked to become king, but he refused.

- **On 15 March 44BC** – called the Ides of March – Caesar was stabbed to death as he entered the Senate. His assassins were a group led by Brutus and Cassius, who felt that his ambitions were a threat to Rome.

The Guptas

- **The Guptas** were a family of rulers who reigned in northern India from AD320-c.500. This is India's golden age, with writing, sculpture and other arts at their peak.

- **The Guptas** were originally a family of rich landowners, who took over control of the small kingdom of Magadha in the Ganges valley.

- **Chandragupta I** came to the throne in AD320. He widened his lands by marrying the right women.

- **Chandragupta's** son Samudragupta and his grandson Chandragupta II gained control over much of northern India by military conquests.

- **The Hindu and Buddhist** religions both began to flourish during the Gupta period.

- **Beautiful temples** and religious sculptures were created all over northern India.

- **About AD450,** Kalidása, India's greatest poet and dramatist, wrote his famous play *Sákuntala*, filled with romance and adventure.

- **Music and dance** developed their highest classical form.

- **Hindu mathematicians** developed the decimal system (counting in tens) that we use today.

- **Gupta power** collapsed by about AD500 under repeated attacks by Huns from the north.

▼ *The Hindu and Buddhist sculpture and painting of the Gupta period has been the model for Indian art down the centuries.*

Gauls and Franks

- **The Gauls** were a Celtic people who lived in Western Europe, mainly in France.

- **The Gauls** could be brave warriors, and because the men had long hair and beards, the Romans thought them wild.

- **In 390BC,** Gauls crossed the Alps, swept down on Rome and sacked the city. They later withdrew, but they occupied northern Italy for almost 200 years.

- **In 278BC,** Gauls invaded what is now Turkey, settling the area called Galatia.

- **In the 50s BC,** Julius Caesar led a lightning Roman campaign to crush the Gauls. What is now France became Roman Gaul.

◀ In 52BC, the Gallic chief Vercingetorix led a last-ditch attempt to drive out the Romans. But he was beaten, taken to Rome as Caesar's prize and executed.

- **The Franks** were a German people split into two branches, the Salians and Ripurians.

- **In AD486,** Clovis, a king of the Salian Franks, invaded Roman Gaul to create a big kingdom covering modern France and Belgium.

- **The first period** of Frankish rule in Gaul is called Merovingian (from 486 to 751); the second is called Carolingian (751-987).

- **After Clovis's death** in 511, the Merovingian kingdom was divided and weakened. About 719, some Merovingian kings allowed a man called Charles Martel – *martel* means hammer – to take control in the north as 'Mayor of the Palace'. Martel soon controlled the whole of Gaul.

> ★ STAR FACT ★
> Franks were outnumbered 20 to 1 by Gallo-Romans – but France is named after them.

Early African civilizations

- **The first civilizations** appeared in Africa along the Nile valley, in Egypt and further south in Nubia.

- **The first Nubian civilization,** called the A-group culture, appeared about 3200BC in the north of Nubia, known as Wawat. It was taken over by the Egyptians in 2950BC.

- **About 2000BC,** a new Nubian culture emerged in the then-fertile south, called Kush. Unlike the Wawat Nubians, who were Asian, the Kushites were black Africans.

◀ Africa was the birthplace of humanity, and rock paintings dating back 30,000 years are found all over Africa.

- **Egypt** conquered Kush in 1500BC, but the Kushites, led by King Shabaka, conquered Egypt in 715BC. For 50 years, the Kushites were pharaohs and their capital Napata was the centre of the ancient world.

- **In 666BC, Assyrians** drove the Kushites out of Egypt. But from the Assyrians, the Kushites learned iron-making.

- **Napata** had iron-ore, but little wood for smelting the ore. So the Kushites moved their capital to Meroe, where they built great palaces, temples, baths and pyramids.

- **From Kush,** iron-making spread west to Nigeria.

- **From AD100, the city of Axum** – now in northern Ethiopia – grew rich and powerful on ivory. About AD350, the Axumite king Aezanas invaded and overthrew Kush.

- **Kings of Axum** (later Ethiopia) were said to be descended from Jewish King Solomon and the Queen of Sheba. The Sheba were an Arab people who had settled in Axum.

- **King Aezanas** was converted to Christianity, but for 1,500 years Axum/Ethiopia was Africa's only Christian country.

The Celts

▶ *Created in the early 800s in Iona and Ireland, the Book of Kells is one of the great treasures of Celtic art.*

- **The Celts** are an ancient group of peoples who first appeared in the Danube valley in Germany about 3,300 years ago.

- **The first Celts** are known as the Urnfield culture, because they put their cremated dead in urns.

- **From 800 to 400BC,** Celts spread across northern Europe, taking over what is now France as Gauls, England as Britons and Ireland as Gaels.

- **The first wave** of expansion is called Halstatt culture. With bronze, the Celts developed supreme metal-working skills.

- **c.500BC,** Celts learned to make iron and came into contact with Greeks and Etruscans. The 'La Tene' culture emerged.

- **In La Tene,** the distinctive Celtic swirls and spiral decoration appeared on weapons and ornaments.

- **After Gauls** sacked Rome, in 390, it seemed Celts might over-run Europe. But they were split into many tribes, and from 200BC they were pushed ever further west.

- **Some early Celts** used Greek letters to write in their own language, but our knowledge of them comes mostly from Greek and Roman authors.

- **The Celts** were fierce warriors who charged into battle shouting, naked and stained with blue woad dye. But they valued poets higher than warriors. Their poets' tales of heroes and magic tell us how rich their culture was.

- **Celtic clan society** was highly organized and revolved around a clan's chief, who made the laws.

The first Britons

- **Britain** has been inhabited by human-like creatures for over 500,000 years. The oldest known settlement, at Star Carr in Yorkshire, dates back 10,000 years.

- **About 6-7,000 years ago,** Neolithic farmers arrived from Europe. They began to clear the island's thick woods to grow crops and build houses in stone.

- **The early farmers** created round monuments of stones and wooden posts called henges. The most famous is Stonehenge in Wiltshire.

- **c.2300BC,** new people from the Rhine arrived. They are called Beakerfolk, after their beaker-shaped pottery cups. They were Britain's first metal-workers.

- **Legend has it** that the name Britain came from Brutus, one of the sons of Aeneas, who fled from Troy.

- **c.700BC,** Celts arrived, often living in hillforts.

- **Iron axes** and ploughs enabled huge areas to be cleared and farmed, and the population rose.

- **When Julius Caesar** invaded, in 55 and 54BC, the Celtic people of England, called Britons, were divided into scores of tribes, such as the Catuvellauni and Atrebates.

- **Resistance** from tribal leaders such as Caratacus meant it took the Romans over a century to conquer the Britons.

- **The last resistance** was that of Queen Boudicca, in AD60.

▼ *People of Bronze Age Britain lived in round houses like this, with thick stone walls and a steeply-pitched, thatched roof.*

A central hearth kept the house remarkably warm

The fall of Rome

- **After the death** of Marcus Aurelius, in AD180, Rome was beset by political struggles.

- **The Praetorian Guard** (the emperor's personal soldiers) chose or deposed emperors at will, and there were 60 emperors between AD235 and 284 alone.

- **The Empire fell** into anarchy and was beset by famine, plague and invasion.

- **Diocletian** (emperor from 284) tried to make the empire easier to govern by splitting it in two halves – East and West. He asked Maximian to rule the west.

- **Diocletian** retired 'to grow cabbages' at his palace in Dalmatia, and soldiers tried to choose a new emperor.

- **Constantine,** commander of the Roman armies in Britain, defeated his rivals to become emperor. It is said that before the main battle, he saw a Christian cross in the sky. After his victory, he became Christian.

- **In AD330,** Constantine made Byzantium (now Istanbul) his capital and called it Constantinople.

▶ After the emperor Constantine moved his capital there in AD330, Byzantium (now Istanbul in Turkey) became the main defender of Roman civilization.

- **After Constantine's death,** the empire fell into chaos again. It became split permanently into East and West.

- **The Western empire** suffered attacks from barbarians. Vandals invaded Spain and North Africa. Goths and Huns such as Attila attacked from the North.

- **In AD410,** Visigoths led by Alaric invaded Italy and sacked (burned and looted) Rome. In AD455, Vandals sacked Rome again. In AD476, the Western empire finally collapsed.

The spread of Christianity

- **The first Christians** were Jews in Palestine, but followers like Paul soon spread the faith to gentiles (non-Jews) and countries beyond Palestine.

- **At first,** Roman rulers tolerated Christians, but after AD64, they saw Christians as a threat and persecuted them.

- **Persecution** strengthened Christianity by creating martyrs such as St Alban.

◀ Early Christian texts were manuscripts (handwritten) and monks spent years illuminating (decorating) them. The illuminated manuscripts of this time are among the most beautiful books ever made.

- **In 313,** Emperor Constantine gave Christians freedom of worship and called the first great ecumenical (general) church council in 325.

- **By 392,** Christianity was the official religion of the empire.

- **When the Roman Empire** split into East and West, so too did Christianity, with the West focused on Rome and the East on Constantinople.

- **The head of the Western church** was the pope; the head of the Eastern church was called the patriarch. The first pope was Jesus's apostle St Peter, and there has been an unbroken line of popes ever since. But the power of the popes really began with St Gregory, in 590.

- **To separate themselves** from the official religion, some Christians, such as St Benedict, began to live apart as monks in monasteries.

- **After AD500,** monks spread Christianity over NW Europe.

- **Monasteries** became the main havens for learning in the West in the Dark Ages, which followed the fall of Rome.

The Byzantine Empire

The Hippodrome was based on the Circus Maximus in Rome

60,000 spectators watched chariot races here

Four great bronze horses by the emperor's seat at the Hippodrome were stolen by Crusaders and are now on St Mark's Cathedral, Venice

Incredibly thick walls protected the city

A massive aqueduct (water channel) kept the city well supplied with water

The Hagia Sophia, now a museum, is the world's oldest Christian cathedral

▲ At its height, Constantinople was graced by some of the ancient world's most magnificent buildings – including the Hippodrome and the Hagia Sophia. This is the tranquil palace quarter. The rest of the city was noisy and crowded.

> ★ STAR FACT ★
> 29 of Byzantium's 88 emperors died violent deaths, and the endless conspiracies at court have given us the word Byzantine for dark intrigues.

- **When Rome collapsed,** in 476, Constantinople (now Istanbul in Turkey) became the capital of what is now called the Byzantine Empire. It became the centre of Western civilization for the next thousand years.

- **In the six years** after Constantine made Byzantium his capital Constantinople, builders, architects and artists created one of the world's most magnificent cities.

- **Constantinople** was at the focus of trade routes between Asia and Europe. Silks, gems and ivories were traded for gold, grain, olives and wine. By charging ten per cent on all goods coming in and out, the city became fabulously rich.

- **When the great emperor Justinian I** came to the throne in 527, he tried to rebuild the Roman Empire. His general, Belisarius, reconquered Italy, and by 565 the Byzantine Empire stretched right round the Mediterranean.

- **Justinian** also built hundreds of churches, including the famous Hagia Sophia.

- **Justinian** modernized Roman law to create the basis of all western legal systems. This is called the Code of Justinian.

- **The Byzantine Empire** was under constant attack – from Goths, Huns, Persians, Avars, Bulgars, Slavs, Vikings, Arabs, Berbers, Turks, Crusaders and Normans. But it repelled attackers, often with its secret weapon 'Greek fire', invented in 650. This was a mix of quick-lime, petrol and sulphur, which burst into flames when it hit water.

- **In 1204,** Constantinople was ransacked by Crusader knights who were short of money. Almost every treasure in the city was stolen and it never recovered from this devastating blow. The city's population dwindled from 1 million to just 60,000 over the next 200 years.

- **Constantinople** was finally conquered by the Turkish Sultan Mehmet II in 1453.

▶ Justinian I was the greatest Byzantine emperor, although his general's secretary, Procopius, described him as 'a demon incarnate'. He ruled with his beautiful former actress wife, Theodora. Justinian relied on her for support and advice, and it was she who changed laws to improve the lives of women and the poor.

The Sui, Tang and Song

▶ *Gunpowder was invented in the Tang era. The Chinese used it first to make fabulous fireworks and later weapons.*

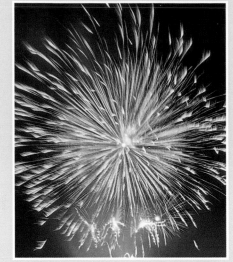

- **In AD581** Yang Chien seized the throne in the north of China, founding the Sui dynasty.

- **Yang Chien** conquered the south and reunited China for the first time since the fall of the Han in AD220.

- **Under the second** Sui emperor Yang Di, China's Grand Canal was rebuilt on an huge scale, linking China's main rivers. Other canals extended the network.

- **Yang Di** was betrayed by one of his 3,000 mistresses and strangled in 618. Li Yuan, an ambitious Sui minister, then seized the throne to found the Tang dynasty.

- **Under the Tang** trade grew, China became rich again and the arts and sciences flourished.

- **By AD751** China was the world's largest empire and the capital Chang'an was the world's largest city, with over a million inhabitants.

- **Chinese people** began to drink tea and sit on chairs.

- **Poets such** as Li Po (701-762) wrote of his love of wild mountains and the fleeting nature of happiness. China's tradition of great landscape painting began and the first printed book, *The Diamond Sutra*, was made in AD868.

- **By AD800,** the Tang dynasty was beginning to break up, Chang'an declined and China descended into turmoil.

- **Order was restored** in AD960 when the Song family began to rule from the city of Kaifeng. The Song lasted until AD1276, when the Mongol Kublai Khan conquered China.

Barbarians

▶ *Alaric was the great Gothic leader who took Rome in 410. He lies buried with the treasures he took from Rome in the bed of the Busentius River.*

- **Barbarians** is what the Romans called all the peoples living outside the empire, who they thought of as uncivilized.

- **Barbarian** people rarely lived in large towns. Instead they lived in forts or small farming villages.

- **Many were brave warriors** but many too were skilled craftsmen, poets and humble farmers.

- **The Romans** thought barbarians wild and crude, but they survived and built a lasting civilization as the peoples of northern and western Europe.

- **They seemed** ill-disciplined in battle to the Romans, but rode horses and appeared in vast, wild, terrifying hordes.

- **The Goths** were German peoples who overran the western Roman empire in the 4th and 5th centuries. They were divided into Ostrogoths in the east near the Black Sea and Visigoths on the Danube. It was the Visigoths who under their king Alaric finally broke Rome in AD476.

- **Italians later** used the term *gothic* to sneer at what they saw as the ugly cathedrals of northern Europe and the term stuck.

- **The Vandals** were a German tribe who arrived in Europe from the east in the 1st century BC. When driven west by the Huns in c.AD380, they took over Spain and North Africa.

- **Vandals** swept down through Italy in AD455 to sack Rome and gave us the word 'vandal'.

- **The Huns** were nomadic Mongols from eastern Asia who arrived in Europe c.AD370, driving everyone before them, until finally defeated in AD455. The Huns were bogeymen for Romans. One Roman said, 'They have a sort of shapeless lump, not a face, and pinholes for eyes' – perhaps because Huns bandaged children's skulls to deform as they grew. The most feared Hun was Attila.

Roman Britain

- **The Roman occupation** began in earnest when the armies of Claudius landed at Richborough in Kent in AD43. All of England and Wales was conquered by AD78.

- **Scotland** remained beyond Roman control. In AD122-130 the 118-km-long stone wall now called Hadrian's wall was built right across the country to act as a frontier.

- **The Roman army** in Britain was powerful. There were three legions (5,000 men each) at York, Chester and Caerleon, plus 40,000 auxiliaries.

- **Roman Britain** was ruled by a Roman governor, but the Romans co-opted local chiefs to help.

- **The Romans** built the first proper towns in Britain – like St Albans, Gloucester and Lincoln – with typical Roman features such as baths and theatres.

- **Demand** for food and leather from the army and the new towns boosted farming. Large estates centred on Roman-style villas grew rich, but even small farmers did well.

- **Most people** were bilingual, speaking and writing both Celtic and Latin, and many adopted Roman lifestyles.

- **When barbarians** attacked the empire on the continent in the AD300s, Roman Britain was left to fend for itself. Power fell into the hands of tyrants like the British king Vortigern (AD425-250).

  - **Vortigern** invited Anglo-Saxons from Germany to settle in the east to help him against rebel Britons. But the Anglo-Saxons soon turned against him and invited in others of their kind to join them.

    - **Villas** and towns were abandoned and Britons fled west or abroad as the Anglo-Saxons moved in.

◄ *King Arthur became the greatest hero in British legend, but the real Arthur was probably a British chief who, for a while, turned the tide against the Anglo-Saxons with a victory at Mt Badon in 500.*

Muhammed

> ★ **STAR FACT** ★
> The Muslim year begins with the day of Muhammed's escape to Medina, called the *Hegira*.

- **Muhammed** (c.570-632) was the Arab prophet whose teachings form the basis of the Islamic religion.

- **Muslims** believe Muhammed was the last and greatest prophet of God, who they called Allah.

- **Muhammed** was born in Mecca in Arabia.

- **His father** died before he was born and his mother died when he was a child. He was brought up by his grandfather and uncle, tending sheep and camels.

- **At the age of 25,** Muhammed entered the service of a rich widow of 40 called Khadija and later married her. They had two sons and four daughters.

- **When 35** Muhammed was asked to restore a sacred stone damaged in a flood. A vision told him to become a prophet and proclaim the word of God.

- **The people of Mecca** resented Muhammed's preaching, and in AD622 he fled to Medina.

- **In Medina** he attracted many followers. The Meccans went to war on Medina, but were driven back.

- **In AD630** Muhammed re-entered Mecca in triumph, pardoned the people and set up a mosque there.

▼ *The Koran is Islam's holy book of Muhammed's teachings.*

What people wore

◄ Egyptians wore clothes made mainly of white linen. At first, men wore a short kilt, but later they wore long, wrap-around skirts. Egyptian women at first wore sheath-like dresses. After 1500BC, men and women both wore loose robes like these made from rectangles of cloth instead.

▼ Roman clothing was quite similar to the Greeks'. Men and women wore tunics, called stola (women) or tunica (men). Citizens of Rome were allowed to wear a carefully draped cloth called a toga over their tunic.

◄ Greek clothes were very simple – essentially just pieces of wool or linen wrapped round to make a tunic, dress or cloak. Young Greek men typically wore a short cloak called a chlamys over a tunic sewn up at the side and fastened at the shoulder. Women wore a dress called a chiton, made from a rectangle of cloth. They wore a longer cloak called a himation.

► In the north of Europe, Celtic peoples wore warm clothes made mainly of dyed wool and leather. Women wore thick dresses and headscarfs. Men wore long tunics, leggings and a cloak.

- **The earliest people** wore animal skins to keep warm.

- **The oldest signs** of woven cloth are marks in clay at Pavlov in Czechoslovakia, which date back 26,000 years.

- **Most of our knowledge** of ancient costumes comes from vases, statues and wall paintings. Colours have often faded, but we know from paintings such as those in the Roman city of Pompeii, preserved under volcanic ash, that ancient clothes were often colourful.

- **The oldest surviving clothes** come from Egyptian tombs dating back 5,000 years.

- **The deep blue** dye indigo, from the indigo plant, has been found in Egyptian cloth from 4,400 years ago.

- **Tyrian purple** was a purple dye, much-prized in ancient times. It came from Tyre (modern Lebanon) and was made from the *Purpura* and *Murex* snails.

- **People such as** the Ancient Egyptians often wore simple sandals or shoes of papyrus or leather. But the Greek dramatist Aeschylus is said to have invented the platform shoe, with 8-cm heels.

- **Minoan women** of 3,500 years ago, unusually for ancient times, wore tight-waisted dresses. Their breasts were also left exposed.

- **Ordinary Roman citizens** wore an unbleached white toga. Coloured borders showed a particular status. Public officials at functions had togas with purple borders, called a *toga praetexta*. Early Roman generals wore togas dyed in Tyrian purple. From the time of Augustus, only the emperor wore a purple toga.

Monks and monasteries

- **In religions** like Christianity and Buddhism, some devout people step out of ordinary life and live in a monastery, a community devoted entirely to religion.

- **The earliest Christian** monastery was that of the hermit St Anthony of Thebes, who went to live in the Egyptian desert about 271, and attracted followers.

- **Basil the Great** (c.329-379) and his sister Macrina the Younger founded monasteries for men and women on their estate in Cappadocia in Turkey.

- **Monasticism** spread rapidly throughout the Byzantine Empire between the 4th and 7th centuries.

- **In the West,** monasticism grew more slowly, so St Martin of Tours (316-397) sent out monks to start new communities. They were very successful in Britain and Ireland.

- **British and Irish** monasteries such as Lindisfarne and Malmesbury were centres of learning in the Dark Ages.

- **The most famous** scholar monk was St Bede of Jarrow (c.672-735), known for his history of the English people.

▶ British and Irish monks laboured to create beautiful illustrated books by hand. This is the Lindisfarne Gospel.

- **The most famous** British monastery was the Scottish Isle of Iona, set up by St Columba in 563.

- **St Benedict** (c.480-547) developed a particular way of living for monks at Monte Cassino in Italy. By 1000, most monasteries followed Benedictine rules.

- **Monasteries** were very vulnerable to Viking raids. Monks were often killed and many treasures lost, and so the monastic life lost some of its attraction.

The spread of Islam

- **Muslims** believe that their religion began the day a prophet named Mohammed left Mecca in AD622, but it was after his death in 632 that it really began to grow.

- **The spread of Islam** was led by caliphs (which means rightly guided).

- **Islam** expanded by conquest, and many peoples only

▼ The Dome of the Rock in Jerusalem, built by Abd al-Malik, was one of the first of many beautiful buildings created by Muslims.

became Muslims after they were conquered. But Muslim conquerors were tolerant of other religions.

- **The Muslims** regarded a conquest as a *jihad* (holy war) and this gave them a powerful zeal.

- **The Muslim Arabs** conquered Iraq (637), Syria (640), Egypt (641) and Persia (650).

- **By 661,** the Islamic Empire stretched from Tunisia to India. Its capital was Damascus.

- **The first Muslims** were Arabs, and as Islam spread, so did Arabs, but the empire contained many peoples.

- **Mohammed** commanded men to 'seek knowledge, even as far as China'. Many Muslims became great scholars.

- **Arts and sciences** flourished under Islam to make it the most cultured, advanced society in the world.

> ★ STAR FACT ★
> In just 100 years, the empire of Islam became bigger than the Roman Empire at its height.

The Fujiwaras

▲ Life at the Fujiwara court was very cultured, with lots of poetry and music. But it was very formal too, with rules for everything.

- **The Fujiwaras** were the family who dominated Japan for five centuries from the 7th century.

- **The Fujiwaras' power** really began in 858, when Fujiwara Yoshifusa married the old emperor. When he died, Yoshifusa became regent to their young son.

- **The Fujiwaras** kept their position by marrying more daughters to emperors, and creating the role of all-powerful *kampaku* (chancellor).

- **The Fujiwara** *kampaku* or regent ran the country while the emperor dealt with religious matters.

- **Fujiwara power** peaked with Michinaga (966-1028).

- **Michinaga's mansions** were more splendid than palaces and filled with banquets, concerts, poetry and picnics.

- **Many women were** novelists and poets, and love affairs were conducted via cleverly poetic letters.

- **The brilliant** court life of Michinaga was captured in the famous novel *The Tale of Genji* by the lady Murasaki.

- **During Michinaga's** reign, warrior families gained the upper hand by quelling rural rebellions, so bringing about the Fujiwaras' downfall.

> ★ STAR FACT ★
> Sei Shonagon, a lady at Michinaga's court, wrote a famous *Pillow Book* – a diary about what she saw.

Anglo-Saxons

- **The Angles, Saxons** and Jutes were peoples from Denmark and Germany who invaded Britain and settled there between AD45 and 600.

- **The Britons resisted** at first, but by 650, they were driven back into the west or made slaves.

- **The Angles** settled in East Anglia and the Midlands, the Saxons in Sussex, Essex and Wessex (Dorset and Hampshire).

◀ In 1939, the burial ship of the overlord Raedwald (died 625) was discovered at Sutton Hoo in East Anglia. This helmet is one of the treasures it held.

- **Each tribe** had its own kingdom, yet by 700 most people in the south thought of themselves as English.

- **Seven leading kingdoms** formed a heptarchy: Essex, Kent, Sussex, Wessex, East Anglia, Mercia and Northumbria.

- **One king** was *bretwalda* (overlord), but the kingdoms vied for power.

- **When Ethelbert of Kent** was *bretwalda*, in 597, St Augustine converted him to Christianity. Christianity spread rapidly throughout England. English monasteries became the universities of Europe. Masons from Gaul and Rome built stone churches.

- **Some Anglo-Saxons** were farmers. Others were warriors as their famous epic poem of heroism, *Beowulf*, shows.

- **In the 700s, Danish raiders** conquered all of England but Wessex. They were pushed back by King Alfred, but attacks resumed in the reign of Ethelred II (978-1016).

- **The last Anglo-Saxon king** was Ethelred II's son, Edward the Confessor (1042-1066).

Bulgars

▶ In the 800s, the Bulgars were converted to Christianity and adopted the Eastern Orthodox church of the Byzantines. They began to create icons like this.

- **The Bulgars** were an Asian people who arrived in Europe on the Volga River c.AD370.

- **The Bulgars** were skilled horse warriors ruled by *khans* (chiefs) and *boyars* (noblemen).

- **The Bulgars** attacked the fringes of the Byzantine Empire until they were in turn attacked by another Asian people called the Avars.

- **After Kurt** became the Bulgar Khan in 605, the Bulgars re-established themselves on the steppes, but when Kurt died, the Bulgars split into five hordes.

- **Four of the five** Bulgar hordes vanished from history, but the fifth was led by Asparukh Khan, west into the Danube valley. Here they overpowered the Slavs living there to create a Bulgarian Empire.

- **Bulgarian Khans** were called caesars or czars after helping Byzantine Emperor Justinian II in 710.

- **The Bulgars** were more often at odds with the Byzantines. They were usually beaten, but after one victory, Krum Khan (803-814) lined Byzantine Emperor Nicephorus's skull with silver to make a drinking cup.

- **The Byzantines** sent St Cyril and his brother St Methodius to convert the Bulgars to Christianity. They succeeded when Czar Boris I was baptized in 864.

- **St Cyril** invented the Cyrillic alphabet, used by Russians and other eastern Europeans today.

- **The Bulgarian Empire** peaked under Simeon I (893-927). Its capital, Preslav, matched Constantinople in splendour.

The caliphs

- **The caliphs** were the rulers of Islam. The word caliph means 'successor', and they were all meant to be successors of Muhammed after he died in AD632.

- **The first caliph** was Muhammed's father-in-law, Abu Bakr. After that came Umar, Uthman and Ali.

- **The first four caliphs** are called the Rashidun ('perfect') because they were the only caliphs accepted by everyone.

- **When Ali died,** in 661, Islam was torn apart by civil war. Some Muslims, called Shi'ites, saw only Ali's successors, the imams, as leaders. Most Muslims followed the Umayyad family, who became caliphs in Damascus.

- **The 14 Umayyad caliphs** expanded the Islamic Empire by conquest through North Africa and into Spain. But it proved too much for them to handle.

- **In 750** the last Umayyad caliph, Marwan II, was beaten at the Battle of the Great Zab by the rival Abbasids, who were descended from Muhammed's uncle.

- **The 38 Abbasid caliphs** turned their eyes eastwards and made a new capital at Baghdad, which soon became the richest city in the world.

- **Under the Abbasids,** Islam became famous for its science, learning and art, especially during the time of Harun al-Rashid.

- **One Umayyad** escaped to set up a rival caliphate in Spain (756–1031).

- **Descendants** of Muhammed's daughter Fatimah became caliphs in Egypt, creating the great city of Cairo.

▶ Under the Abbasid caliphs, Islamic artists made strikingly beautiful ceramic tiles and glassware.

Alfred the Great

- **Alfred the Great** (AD849-899) was the greatest of the Anglo-Saxon kings.

- **Alfred** became king of Wessex in 871 at a time when the Danes had over-run East Anglia, Northumbria and Mercia.

- **In 878,** a series of ferocious Danish attacks drove Alfred to hide on the isle of Athelney in the Somerset marshes.

- **While on the run,** Alfred is said to have hidden in a pigherd's cottage. He was so tired he fell asleep by the fire, letting some cakes burn. Not realizing he was the king, the pigherd's wife scolded him.

- **From Athelney,** Alfred secretly assembled an army and emerged to score a decisive victory over the

> ★ **STAR FACT** ★
> Alfred translated many books from Latin into English so that his people could read them.

◄ *This enamel and gold jewel was found near Athelney. It is inscribed with the words Aelfred me ech eh t gewyrcan – Old English for 'Alfred ordered me to be made'.*

Danes at Edington. The Danes agreed to withdraw to East Anglia and their king Guthrum became a Christian.

- **In 886,** Alfred recaptured London and forced the Danes to stay within an area called Danelaw.

- **Alfred built forts,** reorganized his army and also created England's first navy to defend against invasions.

- **Alfred was a** wise and kindly king who created sound laws, protected the weak from corrupt judges and created laws to help the poor and needy.

- **Alfred was a scholar** who encouraged learning. He decreed that all young men should learn to read English, and made important books available in English.

The Berbers

- **The Berbers** were the people who lived in North Africa before other peoples arrived.

- **'Berber'** comes from *barbara*, Roman for barbarians.

- **Numidian Berbers** allied themselves with Carthage (in what is now Tunisia), the city created when Phoenician traders from Lebanon settled there 3,000 years ago.

- **The Berbers** lived with first Carthaginian, then Roman, Vandal and Byzantine invasions by withdrawing south into the desert, staying as bands of marauders.

- **In the 7th century,** Islamic Arabs invaded North Africa and many Berbers became Muslims.

- **The Berbers** kept their independence by changing Islam to their own tastes. They based their religion on marabouts, holy men who lived very frugally and morally.

- **After 740,** Berbers took back control of North Africa from the Umayyad caliphs.

- **The Berbers** built empires extending into Spain under the Almohads (1121-1269) and Almoravids (1061-1145).

- **Ibn Tumart** was the first Almohad leader, from c.1121. He claimed to be the Mahdi, the holy man whose coming was predicted by Mohammed.

- **The Berber empires** fell to the Arabs in the 12th century.

◄ *When their empires fell, Berbers survived out in the Sahara desert.*

The Vikings

- **The Vikings** were daring raiders from Norway, Sweden and Denmark. Between AD800 and 1100, they swept in on the coasts of northwest Europe in their longships, searching for rich plunder to carry away.

- **People** were terrified by the lightning raids of the Vikings. A prayer of the time went, 'Deliver us, O Lord, from the fury of the Norsemen (Vikings). They ravage our lands. They kill our women and children.'

- **Vikings** prided themselves on their bravery in battle. Most fought on foot with swords, spears and axes. Rich Vikings rode on horseback.

- **Shock troops** called *berserkers* led the attack. *Berserk* is Norse for 'bare shirt' as they wore no armour. Before a battle, they became fighting mad through drink and drugs and trusted in their god Odin to keep them safe.

- **The word** 'Viking' was only used later. People of the time called them Norsemen. The word probably came from Vik, a pirate centre in Norway. When Norsemen went 'a-viking', they meant fighting as a pirate. Swedish Vikings who settled in eastern Europe may have been called *Rus*, and so Russia was named after them.

- **Not all Vikings** were pirates. At home, they were farmers and fishermen, merchants and craftworkers. Many went with the raiders and settled in the north of France, in northern England and in Dublin.

- ▶ The main Viking gods were Odin, Thor and Frey. The Anglo-Saxons had the same gods and their names have given us some days of the week: Odin's or Wodin's day (Wednesday), Thor's day (Thursday) and Frey's or Frigg's day (Friday). Thor's symbol was a hammer called Mjollnir, which caused thunder and lightning. A hammer like this one was used at many stages in a Viking's life – raised over the newborn, laid in the bride's lap at weddings, or carved on a gravestone.

- **The Vikings attacked** mainly Britain and Ireland, but raided as far as Gibraltar and into the Mediterranean.

- **In Eastern Europe,** the Vikings' ships carried them inland up various rivers.They ventured far through Russia and the Ukraine, sometimes marauding as far south as Constantinople, which they called 'Miklagard', the big city.

- **The Norsemen** who settled in northern France were called Normans. The Norman king William the Conqueror, who invaded England in 1066, was descended from their leader, Rollo.

▼ The Vikings were master sailors, and their wooden sailing ships, called longships, are masterpieces of boat-building – light and flat-bottomed enough to sail up shallow rivers, yet seaworthy in the open ocean.

The ships often had a high prow, sometimes carved with a dragon's head

Shields were strapped in rows down each side

When the wind was still, they relied on banks of 20-30 rowers each side

At sea, ships were driven along by a large, square sail made from strips of woollen cloth stitched together

The ships were steered with a large paddle at the rear

★ STAR FACT ★
In November 885, Count Odo and 200 knights fought heroically to defend Paris against Viking hordes but the city was reduced to ashes.

The first Russians

- **Little is known** of the earliest days of Russia, because it was inhabited mainly by nomadic peoples who left few records – such as the Cimmerians (1200-700BC) and later Huns and Khazars.

- **In the 800s AD,** Russia was on the major trade route from NW Europe to the world's richest cities – Constantinople and Baghdad.

- **Slavic peoples** set up trading towns such as Novgorod. They traded in amber, furs, honey, wax and wood.

- **From around 860,** Viking adventurers raided and traded in the region. They were known as the Varangian Rus. The most famous of them was Rurik of Jutland, who took over Novgorod.

- **The city of Kiev** grew up further south, on the Dnieper River.

◀ *Kiev, in the Ukraine, was the focus of the first Russian nation, from 900-1100.*

- **Soon** the Varangian 'grand prince' of Kiev ruled over a vast area historians call Kievan Rus. This covered what is now the Ukraine and eastern Russia.

- **In c.970,** the Slavs took over Kiev under Prince Svyatoslav and his son Vladimir.

- **Vladimir** made Kievan Rus the first Russian nation.

- **Legend says** Vladimir sent people to study different religions. Nothing impressed them until they reached the Hagia Sophia in Constantinople. They were so stunned 'they knew not whether they were in heaven or on earth'.

- **Kiev** quickly adopted Byzantine Christianity. Within 50 years it had 200 beautiful churches – including its own Hagia Sophia – and Vladimir was Russia's first saint.

Harun al-Rashid

- **Harun al-Rashid** (766-809) was the most famous of all the caliphs.

- **In Harun's time**, Baghdad became the most glamorous city in the world, famed for its luxury as well as its poetry, music and learning.

- **Harun** was famous far and wide. He sent ambassadors to the Chinese emperor and an elephant to Charlemagne.

- **Harun's wife** Zubaydah would only drink from silver and gold cups studded with gems.

◀ *The magic and romance of Harun's Baghdad is captured in the tales of The Arabian Nights.*

- **Harun** was a great patron of the arts, and gave lavish gifts to poets and musicians. Yet he also enjoyed watching dogs fight – and often had people executed.

- **Stories tell** how Harun would wander in the moonlight with his friend Abu Nuwas, the brilliant poet, as well as Masrur the executioner.

- **Harun** has become famous because he features in the famous collection of 200-odd tales of *The Thousand and One Nights*, or *The Arabian Nights*.

- **The Arabian Nights** includes such famous characters as Aladdin and his genie, Ali Baba and Sinbad the Sailor.

- **The tales** begin with King Shahriyar of Samarkand distraught by his wife's unfaithfulness. He vows to marry a new girl each night and behead her in the morning.

- **The lovely princess Scheherazade** insists on marrying the king, then at night tells him a tale so entertaining that he lets her live another day to finish it. One story leads to another for 1001 nights, by which time the king has fallen completely in love with her.

The Holy Roman Empire

- **The Holy Roman Empire** was a mostly German empire that lasted from 800 until 1806.

- **It began** when Pope Leo III tried to gain the protection of Charlemagne, the King of the Franks, by reviving the idea of the Roman Empire.

- **Pope Leo III** is said to have taken Charlemagne by surprise in St Peter's church in Rome on Christmas Day 800, and to have placed the crown on his head.

- **Charlemagne's Frankish Empire**, including France, Germany and Italy, became the Holy Roman Empire.

- **When Charlemagne died,** in 814, the newborn Holy Roman Empire fell apart.

- **150 years later,** in 962, the German King Otto I gained control of Italy as well as Germany and insisted the pope crown him Holy Roman Emperor.

- **Over the centuries** the empire was continually beset by conflicts with both powerful Germans and the pope.

- **In 1076,** Pope Gregory VII and Emperor Henry IV were

▲ Until 1531, all Holy Roman Emperors were crowned at Aachen in Germany, where Charlemagne built a cathedral and lies buried.

vying for control. Henry's subjects sided with the pope, so Henry had to give way.

- **Gregory** forced Henry to stand barefoot in snow for three days outside his castle in Tuscany to beg for a pardon.

- **The pope's Vatican** and other Italian cities gained almost complete independence from the emperor.

The Toltecs

> ★ STAR FACT ★
> The name *Toltec* has many meanings: 'cultured person', 'city-type' and 'reed people'.

- **By 900,** the city of Teotihuacán was destroyed and much of Mexico was in the hands of warrior tribes from the north.

- **Legend says** that Teotihuacán was destroyed by one of these warrior tribes called the Toltecs, led by their ruler Mixcóatl. *Mixcóatl* means 'Cloud Serpent'.

- **Under Mixcóatl's son,** Topiltzin, the Toltec were said to have built an empire and also a capital at Tollan, now thought to be Tula, 45 km north of Mexico City.

- **Topiltzin** introduced the cult of the god *Quetzalcóatl* ('Feathered Serpent'), and took the name himself.

- **The Toltecs** were not only great warriors but fine builders and craftsmen. Tollan was full of pyramids, temples and other huge, impressive buildings.

- **Legend says** Tolpiltzin Quetzalcóatl was driven out of Tollan by jealous rivals – including the priests of the god Tezcatlipoca ('Smoking Mirror').

- **After leaving Tollan,** Quetzalcóatl sailed east into the Gulf of Mexico, vowing to return one day.

- **The Aztecs** were greatly influenced by the Toltecs. The Aztecs got the idea of human sacrifices from the priests of Tezcatlipoca. Some Aztecs believed that, when the Spanish arrived in 1519, it was Quetzalcóatl returning in vengeance.

- **The Toltec Empire** broke up in the 12th century and Tollan vanished.

▶ Toltec temples in Tollan were guarded by stone statues of warriors such as this.

The Maoris

▲ The Maoris lived mostly near the coast or by rivers and travelled in light, swift canoes.

- **The early Polynesian** settlers came to New Zealand by canoe from islands in the Pacific.
- **In c.AD100,** Polynesians called the Morioris came here to settle from the Cook, Marquesas or Society Islands.
- **Maori** tradition tells how the Maoris arrived in waves of migration, beginning about 1150 and ending with the coming of a great fleet from the mythical land of Hawaiki 200 years later.
- **Hawaiki** is thought to be the Pacific island of Tahiti.
- **Archaeologists** have found signs of Maori settlement in New Zealand dating back to AD800 and earlier.
- **The first Maoris** lived mainly by hunting and fishing.
- **Maoris** were skilled woodworkers, building beautiful wooden houses covered in carvings.

- **No human** set foot on New Zealand before around 2,000 years ago.
- **The first settlers** in New Zealand were Polynesians.

> ★ STAR FACT ★
> The first Maoris hunted gigantic, flightless birds called moas, which are now extinct.

Charlemagne

- **In 732,** the Frankish (early French) leader Charles Martel halted the great Muslim invasion of Europe in battle at Tours in central France.
- **Martel's** son Pepin the Short made sure of his family's hold on power in the Frankish kingdom. In 768, Pepin's son Charlemagne became King of the Franks.

- **Charlemagne** (742-814) was the greatest European ruler for 1,000 years after Rome's fall.
- **Charlemagne's** name means Charles the Great.
- **Charlemagne** was a great military leader, taking his armies on 53 successful campaigns. He scored victories against the Moors in Spain, and against Saxons and Avars in central Europe.

- **By 796,** Charlemagne had created an empire joining France, Germany, northern Italy and northern Spain.
- **Charlemagne** was a Christian, and in AD800 the pope made Charlemagne Holy Roman Emperor.
- **Charlemagne** was a great ruler who set up an effective law system and introduced the idea of juries in trials.
- **Charlemagne** knew Latin, German and Greek and encouraged scholarship, helped by the great teacher Alcuin.
- **The palace school** in Charlemagne's capital Aachen was the most important school in Europe.

◄ After his death, many legends grew up about Charlemagne. We know that he must have been a powerful personality. One eyewitness said: 'He had a broad and strong body of unusual height…and strode with a firm step and held himself like a man.'

The Magyars

- **The plains** by the River Danube (an area now in Hungary) were settled early in the history of humankind, but little is known of the area before it formed the Roman provinces Dacia and Pannonia. At this time, it was home to Celts and Slavs.

- **Roman Dacia and Pannonia** fell early to the barbarian invaders – Goths, Huns and Avars.

- **In 796,** the Avars were crushed by Charlemagne.

- **In 892,** another Frankish king called Arnulf asked a people called the Magyars to help him against the Moravians, who now lived on the Danube plain.

- **The Magyars** were a people who lived from 3000BC to 800 on the steppes near Russia's River Don.

- **In 889,** the Magyars had been driven to the edge of their land by a people called the Pechenegs, so they were grateful for Arnulf's call.

- **Led by the legendary Arpad,** the Magyars swept into Hungary and made it their home.

- **In 975,** Arpad's great-grandson Géza became a Christian and began to form the Magyars into the Hungarian nation.

- **Géza's son** Stephen (997-1038) carried on his work and became the first king of Hungary.

- **King Stephen,** also called St Stephen, was crowned by the pope on Christmas Day, AD1000.

▲ *King Stephen is a famous figure in Hungarian history and his crown became the symbol of the nation.*

Viking voyages

- **The Vikings** were great seafarers who made some of the most remarkable voyages of ancient times.

- **The Vikings sailed** east through the Baltic and up the Vistula and Dnieper Rivers.

- **The Vikings** sailed west around the British Isles, south round Spain into the Mediterranean.

- **The most daring** Viking voyages were out across the then-unknown open ocean of the North Atlantic.

- **From 900,** the Vikings sailed to and settled on remote islands to the far north – including Iceland, the Faroes and Greenland.

▶This map shows just some of the remarkable voyages made by the Vikings, and their approximate dates. Names in brackets are the Viking names.

- **About 800,** Vikings led by Ohthere reached the remote Siberian islands of Novaya Zemlya in the Arctic.

- **In 1000,** Bjarni Herjulffson was blown off course sailing home from Greenland and saw an unknown shore.

- **Leif Eriksson** sailed west to find this unknown shore. Sagas tell how he found a new land. The Vikings called it Vinland because it was said to be abundant in 'wine berries'. The wine berries he found were probably cranberries.

- **Most experts** now think Vinland is North America, and Leif was the first European to reach it.

- **In AD1004,** the Viking Thorfinn took 130 people to settle in Vinland and stayed three years. Remains of Thorfinn's settlement were found in 1963 at L'Anse aux Meadows, on the northern tip of Newfoundland.

Famous villains

- **Ancient history** has many famous villains – but most were called villains by their enemies, so we can never be sure just how bad they were.

- **Many of the best-known** villains are Roman, including the Emperors Caligula and Nero and Sejanus, Emperor Tiberius's minister, who is believed to have poisoned Drusus, Tiberius's son.

- **The Emperor Claudius's wife** Messalina (AD22-48) got Claudius to execute any man who resisted her advances. She once made love to hundreds of men in a night.

- **Claudius's fourth wife,** his niece Agrippina (AD15-59), probably poisoned him to make way for her son, Nero.

- **Many stories** are told of the Chinese emperor Shi Huangdi's cruelty, including killing 460 scholars.

- **Artaxerxes** (died 338BC) was the cruel Persian king who ravaged Egypt in 343BC.

- **Artaxerxes** and all his sons but Arses were murdered by his minister Bagoas in 338BC. Bagoas then killed Arses and tried to poison the next king, Darius III. Darius found out and made Bagoas drink the poison himself.

- **Herod the Great** (73BC-4BC) of Judea (modern Israel) was a strong king, but he is known best for the murder of his beloved wife Mariamne in a jealous rage and the Biblical tale of the Slaughter of the Innocents. This tale relates how Herod ordered soldiers to kill all babies in Bethlehem in order to get rid of the infant Jews, who prophets had said would be a threat to him.

- **Pontius Pilate** (AD36) was the Roman governor of Judea who let Jesus be crucified.

- **Theodora** was notorious for her secret police.

◄ History paints Nero (top) and Caligula (left) as real villains.

IN SEX CIRCULOS DIVISI

Viking society

- **Vikings ate** beef, cheese, eggs and milk from their farms, meat from deer, elks and seals caught by hunters and fish such as cod, herring and salmon.

- **Vikings lived** in one-storey wooden houses with slanted roofs of turf or straw and no windows. At the centre was a hearth for warmth and cooking. The man of the house sat on a chair called the high seat; the rest sat on benches.

◄ Viking god Odin was said to ride on the eight-legged horse Sleipnir, accompanied by two ravens that brought him news of any battles.

★ **STAR FACT** ★
Viking villages were ruled by a council called the *Thing* or *Folkmoot*.

- **Viking men wore** trousers and a long-sleeved smock shirt. Women wore long woollen or linen dresses.

- **Viking men** could have two or three wives, but marriages were arranged by parents.

- **A Viking woman,** unusually for the time, could own her own property and divorce her husband.

- *Skalds* (poets) went into battle to report on them in verse.

- **The Vikings** were great storytellers. They told of their adventures in long stories called *sagas*.

- **At first** the sagas were only spoken. From 1100-1300, they were written. The most famous is *Njal's saga*.

- **Vikings** were very religious and had several gods. They believed if they died fighting they would go to Valhalla, a special hall in Asgard, the gods' home.

The first English kings

- **Egbert,** king of Wessex from 802 to 839, became in effect the first king of England when he conquered Mercia at Ellandun in 829. But his rule lasted just a year before the Mercian king Wiglaf claimed Mercia back.

- **For 100 years,** much of England was lost to the Danes, but Alfred the Great's son Edward and his daughter Aethelflaed gradually drove the Danes out by 918.

◄ The city of Winchester in southern England was Alfred the Great's capital, and in his time it became a great centre of learning. Canute also made it his capital, and his son Hardecanute is buried here, with Alfred.

- **England's kingship** really began with Athelstan, who was crowned 'king of all Britain' at Kingston on 4 Sept., 925.

- **Ethelred the Unready** was king of England from 978-1013 and 1014-1016. *Rede* was old English for advice, and his name meant he was always badly advised.

- **Ethelred** created so much distrust among his subjects that the Danes easily re-conquered England in 980.

- **In 1013** Dane Sweyn Forkbeard became king of England.

- **When Sweyn** died, Ethelred made a comeback until Sweyn's son Canute drove him out. Canute became king of England in 1016 by marrying Ethelred's widow, Emma.

- **Canute** ruled well. A story tells how he rebuked flatterers by showing how even he could not stop the tide coming in.

- **After Canute,** in 1035, came his son Hardecanute, who died in 1042. Ethelred's son Edward the Confessor then became king – but the Danes did not want a Saxon king.

- **The Danes** called on their Norwegian allies, led first by Magnus then Harold Hardraada, to win back the throne.

Early Scots

- **The first settlers** came to Scotland around 7,000 years ago, and the remains of their huts can be seen on Skara Brae in Orkney.

- **People called Picts** arrived here shortly before the times of the Romans, who failed to conquer Scotland.

- **The Picts** may have come from the Black Sea region. They got their name from the tattooed pictures on their bodies.

- **Brochs** are 15-m high stone towers built for defence around 100BC – perhaps by ancestors of the Picts.

- **Celts** called Scots came from Dalriada in Ireland in c.470. They soon conquered the west.

- **After St Columba** came to set up Iona monastery in 563, Scotland was slowly converted to Christianity.

- **In 563** Scotland was split into four kingdoms: the Scots' Dalriada in the west; the Picts in the north; the Britons' Strathclyde in the southwest; and Bernicia or Lothian of the Angles in the east.

- **In 685,** the Picts drove out the Angles, and in 863, the Dalriada king Kenneth McAlpin conquered the Picts to create a country called Alba, the first Scotland.

- **In the 900s and 1000s,** many people fought to be king in Scotland. Kenneth III killed Constantine III to become king. Malcolm II killed Kenneth III and Duncan I who followed him was killed by his general Macbeth. Macbeth was killed by Malcolm III.

- **Malcolm III's** wife was Saint Margaret (1045-1093), brought up in Hungary where her father was in exile.

► *Macbeth (died 1057) was the Scottish king who became the basis for Shakespeare's tragedy 'Macbeth'. The real Macbeth killed Duncan in battle, not in his bed as in Shakespeare's play.*

INDEX

ACKNOWLEDGEMENTS

Artists: Vanessa Card, Chris Forsey, Mike Foster, Richard Hook, John James, Roger Kent, Terry Riley, Rob Sheffield, Mike Taylor, Mike White, John Woodcock
The publishers thank the following sources for the use of their photographs:
Page 6 (B/C) Illustrated London News; Page 11 (B/C) Lowell Georgia/CORBIS; Page 17 (B/R) Vanni Archive/CORBIS; Page 19 (B/R) Lindsay Hebberd/CORBIS; Page 20 (B/L) Michael Nicholson/CORBIS; Page 40 (T/L) Staffan Widstrand/CORBIS; Page 47 (B/R) Christel Gerstenberg/CORBIS; Page 49 (B/R) Bojan Brecelj/CORBIS; Page 57 (T/R) Aachen Tourist Board

All other photographs are from MKP Archive.